Italy
Luxury

FAMILY HOTELS
& RESORTS

LEVINSON'S FAMILY GUIDES

MAX PUBLICATIONS, INC.
Alpharetta, Georgia

Acknowledgments

Italy is the first book in our new series of *Luxury Family Hotels & Resorts*. It has been an astounding and gratifying undertaking to see it come to fruition over the past eighteen months.

I wish to extend my heartfelt thanks to all those who helped me with this project. Without their input, assistance, goodwill, and constant support, the publication of *Italy Luxury Family Hotels & Resorts* would not have been possible.

To my husband and publishing partner, David, for his endless passion and acuity; my son Jacob for his entrepreneurial insights and writing contributions; my son Isaac for his boundless enthusiasm and guidance with adventurous travel experiences; and my son Ari for his impeccable artistic sense of design.

I wish to extend a hearty thanks to Brian Bodker, my dear friend from the firm of Bodker, Ramsey, Andrews, Winograd & Wildstein, P.C., who ensured that every step of this project reflected my utmost desire for clarity, honesty, and authenticity.

A big debt of gratitude is also owed to our Partners in Adventure and the owners and managers of our Featured Hotels, Resorts, and Restaurants.

I also wish to gratefully acknowledge the expertise and sage advice of Rob Levin of Bookhouse Group, Inc.

Finally, to the people of Italy itself; it is your kindness, generosity, and love of family that keep us coming back time and again to your magical country.

DEBRA LEVINSON, EDITOR-IN-CHIEF

Dedication

In loving memory of my father, Mandell Weiss, whose passion for travel, food, and people forever inspires me. So, as he would always say when we embarked on another travel adventure with the kids: "Go make memories."

Max Publications, Inc.
825 Malvern Hill
Alpharetta, Georgia 30022
USA: 1-800-258-5268
E-mail: info@italyluxuryfamilyhotels.com
Website: www.italyluxuryfamilyhotels.com

Copyright © 2009 Max Publications, Inc.
All rights reserved.

While every precaution has been taken in the preparation of this book, the publisher assumes no responsibility for errors or omissions, or for damages resulting from the use of information contained herein.

No part of this book may be reproduced or transmitted in any form without permission in writing from Max Publications, Inc.

ISBN-13: 978-0-9633577-5-5
ISBN-10: 0-9633577-5-1

Max Publications, Inc. or DL Services, Inc. shall not be liable for any loss, damage, expense, disappointment or inconvenience suffered by any guest during their stay at any Italy Luxury Family Hotels & Resorts.

The exclusive offers contained within the guidebook are not permitted for use by travel agents, tour operators, or booking agents; they are non-commissioned rates.

Printed in China

Contributor: Rena Distasio has over ten years of freelance writing, editing, and researching experience, and contributes articles and content to a variety of print and Internet publications. She also writes about the food, lifestyle, and culture of the southwestern United States for regional publications like *localflavor*, *New At Home*, and *East Mountain Living*, and is an associate editor for Riverbend Books, an award-winning Atlanta-based publisher of story books for cities across the United States.

Book Designer: With over twenty-five years of graphic design experience and eighteen years specializing in book design, Jill Dible has lent her talents to such publishers as Longstreet Press, Vineyard Stories, Dalmation Press, and the Bookhouse Group. She has also worked on publications for the Federal Reserve Bank of Atlanta, the American Cancer Society, the Arthritis Foundation, Habitat for Humanity, and Atlanta's Piedmont Hospital. Currently, Jill serves as photo editor for Atlanta-based Riverbend Books and is working on a media guide for the University of Georgia Bulldogs.

Wine Expert: Jeff Garris is a serious amateur oenophile, having been on the periphery of wines for more than a decade. His credentials include Officier of the Bailage d'Atlanta of the Chaine des Rotisseurs, a society of gastronomic and wine aficionados that dates to the year 1248, as well as a member of l'Ordre Mondial—the wine arm of the society. Mr. Garris is also the Recording Secretary of the Atlanta Wine Tasting Society, a member of Societé d'Lasserre #G105—Paris, and a member of the Society of Wine Educators. He has achieved Certificates of Excellence from *Wine Spectator* magazine with specialties in Bordeaux, California Cabernet, Tuscany, and Wine & Food Pairing. His wine travels have included extensive travels in the U.S. and France. He has been a contributing writer to such magazines as *Indianapolis Monthly* as well as other industry periodicals.

Contents

- 9 Introduction
- 13 Making Your Way through Italy
- 14 Italy's Major Cities, Provinces, Roads, and Water Features
- 15 Estimated Driving Times
- 16 Major Italian Airport Locations
- 17 Driving Distances
- 19 The Fine Art of Italian Wine
- 23 A Culinary Journey through Italy
- 25 Dining Out in Italy

27 Northern Italy

Grand Hotel Sitea 40 | Grand Visconti Palace 42 | Hotel Ancora 44 | Gruppo Guide Alpine 46 | Hotel Bellevue 48 | Ristorante Baita Ermitage 50 | Hotel Cenobio Dei Dogi 52 | Hotel Elephant 54 | Hotel Portofino Kulm 56 | Hotel Villa Aminta 58 | Hotel Villa Cá Sette 60 | Hotel Villa Franceschi 62 | Hotel Villa Margherita 64 | Locanda Dei Mai Intees 66 | Palazzo Barbarigo Sul Canal Grande 68 | Royal Hotel Sanremo 70 | San Clemente Palace Hotel & Resort 72 | Villa Luppis 74

77 Central Italy

Albergo Del Sole Al Pantheon 90 | Albergo Pietrasanta 92 | Borgo Tre Rose 94 | Castello Di Gargonza 96 | Castello Di Magona 98 | Castello Di Vicarello 100 | Castello Orsini Hotel 102 | Eremo Delle Grazie 104 | Hotel Dei Mellini 106 | Hotel Eden 108 | Hotel Lord Byron 110 | Hotel Palazzo Bocci 112 | Ristorante Il Molino 114 | Hotel Regency 116 | IL Borro 118 | Lucignanello Bandini 120 | Palazzo Viviani 122 | Park Hotel Villa Grazioli 124 | Relais Campo Regio 126 | Relais & Chateaux Villa La Vedetta 128 | Relais La Corte Dei Papi 130 | Residenza Del Moro 132 | Italy Segway Tours 134 | Residenza Torre Di San Martino 136 | Antica Locanda Del Falco 138 | Tombolo Talasso Resort 140 | Villa Campestri 142 | Villa Di Piazzano 144 | Villa Gamberaia 146 | Villa La Massa 148 | Villa Marsili 150 | Ristorante La Bucaccia 152 | Villa Milani 154 | Trattoria La Palomba 156 | Villa Olmi Resort 158

161 Southern Italy

Falconara Charming House & Resort 176 | Forte Village Resort 178 | Hotel Castello at Forte Village Resort 180 | Villa Del Parco at Forte Village Resort 182 | Grand Hotel Excelsior Vittoria 184 | Hotel Cala Caterina 186 | Hotel La Coluccia 188 | Hotel Pellicano D'oro 190 | Hotel Villa Meligunis 192 | Il Melograno Relais & Chateaux 194 | San Domenico Palace Hotel 196 | Sant'Elmo Beach Hotel 198 | Sofitel Thalassa Timi Ama 200 | Tarthesh Hotel 202 | Villa Las Tronas 204

210 Directory

212 Photo Credits

213 Index

"For us to go to Italy is like a most fascinating act of self-discovery—back, back down the old ways of time. Strange and wonderful chords awake in us, and vibrate again after many hundreds of years of complete forgetfulness."

— D. H. Lawrence

INTRODUCTION

One of the great joys of traveling through Italy is discovering firsthand that it is, indeed, a dream destination. Its countryside has long enticed visitors with its timeless beauty, from romantic, undulating plains to majestic Alpine peaks to miles of uninterrupted white beaches. Its cities are both repositories for some of the world's greatest art and architecture, as well as bustling centers of fashion and industry. Likewise, three millennia of traditions have formed distinctive personalities among the Italians themselves, who continue to charm visitors from across the globe with their hospitality and warmth.

Something for Everyone

Each of Italy's twenty diverse regions reveals a rich array of cultural, historical, and culinary delights that will enlighten and enchant travelers of all ages and sensibilities.

For the epicurean, Italy is a marvel of culinary exploration, revealing its treasures in everything from elegant *ristorantes* to family-owned *trattorias*. Wine aficionados will likewise journey through the regions to their hearts' delight, discovering the vast selections that lie ahead. A myriad of adrenaline-rush-inducing adventures, from paddling and rock climbing to Alpine trekking and off-piste skiing, lure extreme sports enthusiasts of all ability levels. Art and history lovers will experience firsthand the breathtaking genius displayed in the works of Leonardo da Vinci, Raphael, Michelangelo, Brunelleschi, and many others. Italy is also a country that reveres children, so youngsters will not only be thrilled to discover gelato, pizza, and pasta, but also beautiful beaches, water parks, and zoos.

A Luxury Family Travel Experience

While there are plenty of magazines and books that cater to singles, couples, and budget travelers, few take into consideration the needs of the traveling family seeking luxury accommodations and authentic, immersive experiences in Italy's foremost destination cities.

Italy Luxury Family Hotels & Resorts guidebook and Web site fill this void by offering a host of luxury accommodations that exemplify the romance for which Italy is famous. Whether planning a dream wedding, sumptuous anniversary party, glamorous getaway, or joyous family reunion full of love and laughter, these are places where you can indulge your sense and truly celebrate *la dolce vita*.

ABOVE: Publishers David and Debra Levinson at Hotel Cenobio dei Dogi on the Italian Riviera. OPPOSITE: Sardinia's Tarthesh Hotel, with its lovely swimming pool and hydrotherapeutic area surrounded by myrtle and palm trees.

Exceptional Accommodations

Italy Luxury Family Hotels & Resorts presents a specially selected group of leading hotels, resorts, villas, historic houses, and castles located in Italy's most preferred destinations. These properties are distinguished by their management's passion for providing unique luxury hospitality experiences for families. Many are renowned

for award-winning or five-star service and amenities. Others have earned distinction for unique features—outstanding views, privileged locations, Gambero Rosso or Michelin star rated cuisine, extensive wine lists, one-of-a-kind antiques, alluring architecture and décor, historical significance, beautiful natural surroundings, and secluded beaches.

Most importantly, each property meets our highest standards for family travel, whether your plans mean you'll need extra cots for the little ones or an entire hotel to house the extended family for a weeklong sojourn.

Using this Guide:

Italy Luxury Family Hotels & Resorts is divided into three sections – Northern, Central, and Southern Italy—each with their corresponding geographical regions, the distinguishing features of those regions, and their individual luxury properties.

Each review provides information on that property's history, its services, amenities, and bars and restaurants, along with suggestions on things to do and see in the surrounding areas. The Special Features at the end of each review provide a quick summary of property highlights, including what our family enjoyed most about our stay and the most appropriate age for children. Unquestionably, every property extends a warm welcome to families, though some are best for grown children, others ideal for those with babies, and others are

THIS PAGE: Breakfast amid a sea of olive trees that surround the 17th-century Masseria (farmhouse) of IL Melograno Relais & Chateaux, which is located in Puglia. OPPOSITE: (TOP & BOTTOM): With twenty-one different restaurants at Sardinia's Forte Village Resort, the whole family, kids included, will always find exactly what they want to eat.

perfect for honeymoons, anniversaries, family reunions, and intimate getaways.

This book is also packed with Exclusive Luxury Family Offers, such as inclusive packages, room rate discounts, free room nights, romantic candlelight dinners, wine and olive oil tastings, spa treatments, museum tickets, and arrival gifts like sparkling wine and fruit baskets and children's gift bags. To take advantage of these and other offers available exclusively to Luxury Family Travelers, please reference code LFHR-09 when you make your reservations.

About the Publisher

We are a dynamic family-run company representing an extraordinary group of select hotels and resorts offering unsurpassed services to an elite clientele. Our first guidebook, *Italy's Best with Kids*, was a self-publishing phenomenon, transcending a humble beginning to end up a brisk seller in major chain bookstores.

With years of travel experience throughout Italy, we have visited, slept in, inspected, eaten at, and developed close, personal relationships with the owners and management of all our choice properties. In our quest to seek out the best Italy has to offer, we have skied the Italian Alps, toured the art centers of Rome, Florence, and Venice, inspected hotel kitchens and assisted with food preparation, sailed the archipelago islands, scuba dived in the Mediterranean, and luxuriated on some of the country's most exclusive beaches.

Because of our relationships with our recommended properties, travelers to Italy often comment that as soon as they identify themselves as a Luxury Family Traveler, they are greeted with extra warm recognition. Time and again these travelers go on to report of special VIP treatments upon arrival, ranging from little extras like early check-ins and late check-outs, to room upgrades and welcome gifts in their rooms upon arrival. These are just a few of the many perks extended to our Luxury Family Travelers.

Join Us!

Italy Luxury Family Hotels & Resorts travel guidebook and Web site reveal select leading hotels, resorts, villas, and castles throughout Italy, for families of all ages who desire unique experiences. Whether you seek travel planning recommendations for the ideal places to sleep and eat while immersed in this outstandingly beautiful country or you would like to become part of the brand as one of our approved Luxury Family Hotels, Luxury Family Partners, or Luxury Family Travel Specialists, we invite you to join our team. Call 1-800-258-5268, or log onto www.italyluxuryfamilyhotels.com to learn more about how you can benefit from our expert knowledge of this endearing country.

Making Your Way through Italy

Designing Your Itinerary

This chapter is designed to assist you with the advanced planning required to develop your ideal and personalized Italy Luxury Family tour. To facilitate your seamless navigation through this diverse country, we have included three large-scale maps: one highlights Italy's major cities, provinces, roads, and water features; the second provides estimated travel times between the most popular destination cities; and the third lists all major Italian airports, where European-based carriers such as Eurofly, Meridiana Air, Ryanair, and Easyjet will easily connect you to all ports throughout the country. In addition, a second distance chart highlights in kilometers the most important point-to-point distances between major cities.

How to Use Maps & Charts

We recommend you begin your planning by reading our "Highlights of the Regions" section, which will provide you with a great overview of Italy, including major cities, surrounding attractions, and places to stay. Say, for instance, your family decides to spend the summer holiday experiencing the exquisite beaches and sights in Sicily. For an overall perspective, view the main map of Italy, which highlights each region's major cities, provinces, roads, and water features. The areas in Sicily you may want to consider visiting are Palermo, Agrigento, and Taormina, with a worthwhile excursion to the Aeolian Island of Lipari. Next, view the estimated time and distance maps, and/or consult the major Italian airports map for the best ports. Most itineraries can be done in reverse, and in many instances you can fly into one port and out of another. Then, visit our Luxury Family Hotels & Resorts contained within this guidebook or visit www.italyluxuryfamilyhotels.com to find the best accommodations in your choice Italy locations.

OPPOSITE: The estate of Villa di Piazzano, located in the countryside on the border between Tuscany and Umbria. THIS PAGE: Publishers David and Debra Levinson sailing the crystalline waters of Tuscany's Archipelago Islands, which feature sandy beaches, numerous inlets, rocky coastlines, and quaint towns.

ESTIMATED DRIVING TIMES

DRIVING DISTANCES
Kilometers between main locations:

Conversion Table
1 Km. = 0.621 mile | 1 mile =1.609 Km.

	Bari	Bologna	Bolzano	Florence	Genoa	Milan	Naples	Palermo	Rome	Turin	Trieste	Venice
Agrigento	703	1314	1571	1202	1437	1504	748	127	958	1600	1599	1460
Ancona	464	226	507	352	529	441	394	1142	306	559	517	378
Aosta	1067	405	456	477	248	186	947	1642	759	114	589	450
Arezzo	645	188	444	75	314	376	416	1109	228	472	473	334
Assisi	548	250	531	173	407	465	385	1079	197	571	484	344
Bari	—	670	948	702	937	882	262	667	432	1000	958	819
Bologna	670	—	287	131	309	221	587	1281	398	339	295	155
Bolzano	948	287	—	386	411	288	842	1537	654	411	365	226
Catania	542	1153	1410	1041	1276	1343	587	210	797	1439	1438	1314
Como	935	273	321	371	191	51	828	1522	639	168	454	316
Cortina	899	291	133	411	540	417	867	1561	678	540	247	160
Florence	702	131	386	—	251	318	473	1168	285	414	413	274
Genoa	882	309	411	251	—	142	712	1407	524	170	537	398
Lucca	776	163	419	77	164	280	547	1241	358	328	448	308
Milan	882	221	288	318	142	—	774	1468	585	142	416	276
Naples	262	587	842	473	712	774	—	714	229	872	871	732
Palermo	667	1281	1537	1168	1407	1468	714	—	922	1564	1563	1424
Parma	766	105	282	203	207	125	660	1352	472	244	388	249
Perugia	566	237	520	151	386	453	372	1066	183	549	470	331
Piacenza	820	159	271	257	152	68	714	1408	525	183	404	265
Pisa	807	194	451	108	170	286	578	1273	334	334	479	340
Reggio Calabria	453	1064	1321	953	1187	1254	499	241	708	1351	1350	1211
Rimini	560	117	398	243	420	331	515	1238	375	450	408	268
Roma	432	398	654	285	524	585	229	922	—	684	683	543
Salerno	242	627	884	515	750	817	56	662	271	913	912	773
Sanremo	1076	430	532	377	148	271	847	1541	659	233	665	526
Siena	660	177	433	75	299	367	431	1125	243	463	462	326
Taormina	496	1107	1364	995	1230	1297	541	261	751	1393	1392	1253
Turin	1000	339	411	414	170	142	872	1564	684	—	545	405
Venice	819	155	226	274	398	276	732	1424	543	405	163	—
Verona	815	153	154	252	295	172	708	1402	519	295	257	118

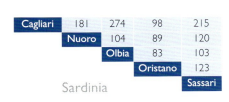

The Fine Art of Italian Wine

In providing a brief insight to Italian wines, one should start by understanding the complex nature of the country and its offerings to the oenophile. Some of the greatest wines of Italy had no legal standing until the mid-1990s, many of its most prestigious producers have also made wines of inconsistent quality, and most of Italy's grapes are unique to the country. Beyond that, some of the highest-rated wines in the world are now produced in Italy, including Ornellaia, Sassicaia, Tignanello, and the wines of Angelo Gaja. The variety and quality of wines produced in Italy also continue to increase and improve dramatically. All of this contributes to a terrific location for anyone who enjoys a taste of the grape, either seriously or occasionally.

Italy continues to be among the world leaders in wine. Based on statistics through 2005, Italy is second in the world (behind France) in the production of wine, third (behind Spain and France) in total area of vineyards, and sixth in the world in per-capita wine consumption, with the Vatican City ranking number one. Imagine that!

There are some nineteen varietals of red grapes (led by Sangiovese and Nebbiolo) and fourteen varietals of white grapes (led by four permutations of Trebbiano) that are widely grown in Italy. Most of these grapes are not in major production in other parts of the world, which means many of Italy's wines have unique flavor characteristics.

Sangiovese is the mainstay grape of Italy. It flourishes in the northern regions, especially in Tuscany where it is the prime ingredient in Chianti and many other wines. At best, it produces wines with bright fruit flavors and very good acidity. In most cases a taster will get notes of cherry and currants in the glass.

Nebbiolo is the most illustrious grape in the Piedmonte region, especially in Barolo and Barbaresco. These are slow-developing wines of intensity, austerity, and refinement. Some are more fruit-forward and can be drunk at a younger age. The upper range of this grape from the better producers provides notes of strawberry, raspberry, and roses with great concentration and the ability to age for substantially more than a decade.

The Trebbiano grape is widely prolific, low in alcohol, and high in acidity. It can be found in virtually any Italian white wine, and is even allowed by law to be blended into Chianti and Vino Noble di Montipulciano, although Tuscan producers seldom follow the practice anymore. In most wines you will find floral hints with honey, lime, and some mineral qualities.

OPPOSITE: The famous wines of Tuscany as displayed in the tasting cellar of Villa di Piazzano. THIS PAGE: In Italy, more so than in much of the world, wine is made to go with food; La Bucaccia Ristorante's wine cellar offers over two hundred different regional wines that servers astutely pair with authentic Tuscan cuisine.

THIS PAGE: Properly pairing wine and cheese is artfully accomplished at Val d'Aosta's Hotel Bellevue. OPPOSITE: Salami, prosciutto, and cheese—an Italian meal wouldn't quite seem the same without this customary antipasti dish, served with a light, fruity red wine. Image courtesy La Bucaccia Ristorante.

Italian Wine Classifications

In 1963, the Italian government established a system of *denominazione di origine*, or denomination of origin, following the lead of the French methodology of categorizing quality production of wine. These laws govern the geographical limits of each wine-producing region, the grape varieties that can be used, the percentages of each grape that can be used in specified blends, the maximum amount of wine that can be produced by acre (hectare), the minimum (but not maximum) alcohol content of the wine, and the aging requirements—whether in glass or in wood. Prior to 2006, only about 10 percent of the entire Italian wine production was regulated by these laws. This continues to change, with new laws incorporating more wines into the categories.

Overall, there are two major categories of wine—quality wine (DOCG and DOC) and table wine (IGT and VdT). DOCG (*Denominazione di Origine Controllata e Garantia*) is the top echelon of Italian wine. Even though the system was established in 1963, there were no DOCG wines acknowledged until 1980.

Today there are some thirty-six wines in this classification, including Barbaresco, Barolo, Brunello di Montalcino, and Vino Noble di Montepulciano. Of these, nineteen are in the area described elsewhere as Northern Italy, including Piedmonte, Lombardia, Veneto, Friuli-Venezia-Giulia, and Emilia-Romagna. The highest category of Italian wines are those that are categorized as DOCG. These have strict guidelines on both the type of grape and the harvest yields, and the wine must be analyzed and tasted by a special panel before achieving DOCG status.

DOC (*Denominazione di Origine Controllata*) applies to wines made from specific varietals grown in specific zones and aged by specific methods. DOC wines do not always guarantee quality, as they tend to protect the more traditional production methods, grapes, geographies, and history. As of 2006, there were more than 300 DOC-classified wines.

IGT (*Indicazione Geografica Tipica*) was created to be the Italian version of the French designation *vin de pays* as a higher level of table or daily wine. These wines typically carry a geographical description on the label, followed by the name of the grape varietal. As some producers have struggled with the DOC classification and may not be eligible for DOCG, some of Italy's greatest wines carry the IGT designation.

VdT (*Vino da Tavola*) is the most basic classification, and there will be no indication on the label of the grape varietal or the geographic production region. This group also does not allow for the listing of the vintage on the label, which forces most producers up at least one level in order to comply with the laws.

Italian Wines and Food

In Italy, more so than in much of the world, wine is made to go with the food. No meal, with the exception of some breakfast items, is served without wine being available, and for good reason. There are so many varietals in Italy, it is difficult to provide a suggestion for each. Here is a representative selection of the more common grapes that may be found throughout the country, along with suggestions for pairing them with food.

These suggestions are based on personal experiences as well as what some producers and other cognoscenti have enjoyed. Please don't accept these suggestions as dictums. Get a bottle of wine, select a tasty dish, *mangi,* and make your own determinations!

Barbaresco – Tailored for veal and meat dishes, pasta with Porcini mushrooms, as well as mature cheeses such as Fontina.

Barbera – Chicken and lighter foods including simply prepared pork.

Barolo – Lamb. Nothing else to be said. Unless you include a roast in its own sauce or meat cooked with the same wine such as wild rabbit, duck, or risotto.

Brunello – Most meat dishes, but especially the stronger ones of grilled steak, wild boar, pheasant, and other game. Great to try with some aged Pecorino Toscano cheese as well.

Dolcetto – First courses of antipasti, including those with tomato sauces and pasta, but not with seafood. Also with strawberries or peaches for dessert.

Nebbiolo – All types of red meat, especially roasts. Also excellent with cold meats such as salami and most hard cheeses.

Trebbiano – Game dishes including rabbit and cubed lamb.

Vermentino – Fish and shellfish of any variety.

A Note about Grappa

Considered Italy's brandy, Grappa is a grape-based spirit of between 80 and 100 proof, made from the distillation of pomace. Pomace (also sometimes called marc) comprises pieces of grapes, including the stems and seeds, which were pressed for the winemaking process. Originally conceived as a way to prevent waste by using leftovers at the end of the wine season, Grappa is currently produced throughout the country and has become commercialized and widely exported.

A Culinary Journey through Italy

Italy is home to exceptional and important museums, ancient ruins, and medieval castles, but there is no doubt that some of its greatest pleasures are to be experienced through its sensational cuisine.

One of the delights of traveling through Italy is the diversity of ingredients and food preparation methods found throughout the regions, all deeply influenced by their past and revealing their own individual gastronomic traditions. Italian cuisine is symbolic of a country that wasn't unified until 1861. Previously, each region produced only its classic cuisine, relying solely on ingredients that could be harvested and cultivated locally. Today, regional products can be shipped all over Italy, but Italians still stay true to their locally produced ingredients, as they choose freshness and quality over a multiplicity of ingredients or the latest culinary trends. Therefore, classic Italian cuisine can only be categorized by one common denominator: incorporation of top-quality ingredients that are omnipresent throughout the country.

As Italy's regional climates and geographical conditions are different from one another, the available products as well as the tastes of the people vary; consequently, recipes that originated in one particular region will have an entirely different style and flavor when prepared in another. Pasta certainly is typical of Italian cuisine, yet each region has its own unique shape and preparation, such as the *trenette* of the Ligurian coast, the *tortellini* of Emilia Romagna, or the *tagliatelle* of Umbria.

The heart of Italian cooking today is still its simplicity; ingredients are used to complement rather than mask the taste of the fresh vegetables, fruits, meats, fish, and even cheeses. For instance, along the seaside, freshly caught fish is usually grilled, then served with a touch of olive oil, lemon, and freshly ground pepper. The succulent blood oranges from Sicily as prepared in *insalata di arance* (orange salad) need nothing more than a little fresh, raw fennel, onions, rosemary, ground pepper, and oil and vinegar as accompaniments. Even pasta is intended to be served with sauces that enhance, not distract from, the pureness of its flavor.

Italian desserts are completely delectable, yet the ingredients blend together so perfectly their parts are indistinguishable from the whole. A good example of this is *panna cotta*, the famous upside-down whipped cream pudding of Emilia-Romagna, which is made with only cream, vanilla bean, gelatin, and sugar as the backdrop to fresh red raspberries and strawberries.

ABOVE: A stay at a Luxury Family Hotels and Resorts property means plenty of opportunities to savor the country's cuisine, like this selection of exotic sweet and savory breakfast items. Image courtesy Villa Marsili, Cortona. OPPOSITE: High above the Umbrian town of Spoleto on the road to Monteluco sits the ancient mountaintop monastery of Eremo delle Grazie, where classic risotto takes on a unique taste all its own with the addition of melon.

THIS PAGE: In Florence at Hotel Regency's restaurant, Relais Le Jardin, the cuisine is distinctly Italian and carefully matched with rare wines selected by the experienced sommelier. OPPOSITE: Eating in Italy is always a luxurious experience, regardless of whether the meal consists of a simple slice of pizza on the street or an elegant sit down dinner; image courtesy Villa di Piazzano, Tuscany.

Many of the hotels and cafes will advertise American breakfast because *colazione* (Italian breakfast) is quite different. *Colazione* is light and traditionally consists of *cappuccino* (concentrated coffee with frothed milk) and a *brioche* (sweet pastry) or just simply an *espresso* (concentrated coffee). Customarily, *pranzo* (lunch) is the largest meal of the day. A traditional Italian meal is orchestrated like a great theatrical production with a series of scenes presented in a succinct order: *antipasto* (starter), a *primo piatto* (pasta, rice, or soup), a *secondo piatto* (meat or fish) with *contorno* (vegetable or salad), then *frutta* (fresh fruit). *Cena* (dinner) is similar to lunch. Today, there is a trend towards having a light lunch with dinner as the main meal. Both meals may be finished with *espresso* and maybe a *grappa*, *amaro* or *limoncello* (digestive liqueur).

Finding a place to eat in Italy is simple, but deciding on food and ambience will vary based on the type of establishment. A *ristoranti* (restaurant) is usually family run, with a more formal décor and meals that tend to last for hours. *Trattorias* and *osteria* are less formal and usually less expensive, serving local specialties. A *panineria* is a sandwich bar, where quick meals can be had the majority of the day. A *pizzeria* is perhaps the most familiar, but in Italy the menu goes beyond pizza to include many of the classically satisfying dishes.

As you are eating your way through Italy you will notice certain select foods such as cheeses and sausages carry a special governmental approved seal, which acknowledges its outstanding regional quality. This is known as the "controlled designation of origin," indicated by the initials DOC. Foods that receive this stamp of approval have met the government's strictest of standards for quality and authenticity. A prime example is *Asiago* cheese from the Veneto region. *Asiago* received its DOC certification in 1978, which not only limited the geographical area in which the milk used in its production could be produced and collected, but also ensured that its traditional production methods were adhered to and carried out. The officially recognized zones are defined as the whole province of Vicenza and Trento as well as the two provinces of Treviso and Padova. *Asiago* also received an additional certification of DOP, or "protected designation of origin," one of only 30 among Italy's 400 or so cheeses to have been awarded this honor.

Regardless of its simplicity or sophistication, whether the products were collected and produced in Piedmonte or Puglia, or its ingredients hold a DOC or DOP certification, Italian cuisine ultimately arouses the senses though its artful expression and the joining together of friends and family.

Dining Out in Italy

Our featured hotels and resorts offer some of the finest award-winning cuisine and dining experiences available in Italy. In fact, the quality and reputation of their restaurants was a major factor in our choosing which hotels to include as part of this exclusive collection. Because of that, our recommendations most often remain narrow beyond our hotels' doors. Nonetheless, we have had several exemplary experiences at outside restaurants, ones we feel are worth the journey for outstanding regional specialties in an atmosphere of equal measure. You will find our reviews of these restaurants after the Featured Hotel and Resort with whom they share the same town, city, or region. For instance, if you are traveling to Spoleto, you will see our featured hotel and resort for that city is the Hotel Palazzo Bocci, and included after its description is our review of nearby Ristorante Il Molino.

Northern Italy

With its diversity of landscapes and cultures, Northern Italy has long been a favorite destination for the adventurous traveler. Within only a few days' time, you can ski towering alpine peaks, navigate the labyrinthine canals of Venice, scout the chic boutiques of Milan, and lounge in luxury at exclusive resorts along the Ligurian Coast. Grand palaces, medieval castles, and innumerable artistic treasures from antiquity to the present day await the intrepid traveler. Food and wine aficionados will have many opportunities to indulge their passions. French and German influences have left their mark not only on the region's wine-making traditions but also on the culinary styles, which range from down home to haute cuisine.

Valle d'Aosta

This region is positioned in the northwestern corner of Italy, and is the country's most mountainous area, entirely surrounded by impressive alpine peaks: Monte Blanc, the Matterhorn, the Monte Rosa, and the Gran Paradiso. Aosta, capital of the region and the only province of the valley, is a city rich in history; the ancient Augusta Pretoria (Latin name for Aosta) is evident in the great Arch of Augustus (25 B.C.) and the remains of the Roman Theatre. It is also one of the best towns from which to explore the mountains and valleys, which offer great hiking, biking, paddling, climbing, and skiing opportunities. The main resorts of the area are Courmayeur and Cervinia, which extends over the border into Switzerland. Others present stunning surroundings along with interesting *pistes* (ski runs) for skiers of all levels. Such destinations include Pila, which is accessible from the town of Aosta by gondola, Gressonney, Champoluc, Alagna, and Valtournenche. This vast snowy area begins at 1,524 meters and eventually climbs to 4,478 meters to the top of the Matterhorn. This region is an enchanting paradise of feudal castles and towers from the Middle Ages, particularly along the Dora Baltea River.

The mountain resort town of Saint-Vincent is a great base from which to tour the many castles of Valle d'Aosta, Casino de la Vallée (one of Europe's largest casinos), mineral water spas,

With 1,200 km of perfectly groomed slopes and guaranteed snow, the Dolomite Mountains provide a stunning setting for a variety of winter sports suitable for the whole family. Pictured from left to right are a few members of the Luxury Family Hotels & Resorts team: Jacob, David, Isaac, and Ari Levinson.

FAMILY HOTELS & RESORTS | 27

OPPOSITE: A vacation in Valle d'Aosta offers visitors the chance to discover a well-preserved land and a people who still cherish their traditional ways of life, which include a genuinely warm, family-style mountain hospitality. THIS PAGE: Villa Aminta was built in the 19th century as an exclusive residence; today it is the most preferred luxury hotel on Lake Maggiore.

the nearby mountains, and Italy's oldest park, Gran Paradiso National Park. Cogne is one of the most beautiful summer mountain villages of the Alps with many inspiring walks and hikes of various degrees of difficulty, leading to lakes and waterfalls. In the winter Cogne offers cross-country and some downhill skiing, snowshoeing, and more than 140 icefalls for ice climbing.

Classic Cuisine: The cuisine of Northern Italy has been influenced by the close proximity of both France and Piedmonte, but maintains its own distinguished character. Rich in dairy products, the region's cuisine functions to generate heat in the alpine climate. Specialties include mushrooms, roasted meats, and cheeses, of which Fontina, produced in the region since the 12th century, is the best known. The Northern Italian version of cheese fondue is a *fonduta,* made with melted Fontina, milk, eggs, and flour. Other local specialties include nourishing soups, stews, risotto, and polenta, as well as *Costoletta alla Valdostana*, a veal chop covered in Fontina.

Divine Wine: The region's best wines include the sparkling Blanc de Morgex et de La Salle and the rare, highly prized ice wine, Chaudelune. The best reds produced here tend to be young and fruity, and also include vintages from the Donnaz (or Donnas) and Enfer d'Arvier localities. The region's primary red grape is Nebbiolo, although it is different in character and taste from the Piedmonte Nebbiolo.

Piedmonte

Like the Valle d'Aosta, this region's appeal lies in its proximity to beautiful alpine landscapes and to France, which has an abundant influence on the region's culinary output. Piedmonte is also an outdoor adventurer's dream, with superb hiking and mountain biking opportunities. Its portion of the Italian lakes includes Lake Orta and the whole western half of Lake Maggiore. Turin, the capital, is a fascinating European city, boasting both a contemporary international flavor and an aura of antiquity. It is home to the much-disputed reproduction of the Holy Shroud in which Jesus was allegedly wrapped after he was removed from the cross. It can be seen on display in the Cathedral of San Giovanni. In Turin, you will also find the Egyptian Museum, holding one of the most important collections of Egyptian artifacts existing outside of Egypt itself. Other noteworthy sites include the extensive weaponry collection housed at the Royal Armory; important Piedmontese, Dutch, and Flemish artwork at the Sabauda Gallery; the Automotive Museum's collection of cars ranging from vintage to modern and concept; and the Royal Palace, built in the 17th century to house the

House of Savoy. Stresa, previously a small fishing village, has developed into a popular tourist area located on one of the most scenic areas of Lake Maggiore. Castles are plentiful throughout the region, lending a fairytale characteristic to their surroundings.

Classic Cuisine: The region's highly prized, rare, and very costly *tartufi bianchi* (white truffles) that grow underground beneath certain oak trees attract food connoisseurs from all over the world. Production is concentrated in and around the small town of Alba, and the fungi are utilized not only in specialty food items like truffle-scented olive oils and truffle-infused cheeses, but also by the world's finest chefs to enrich a variety of pastas, risottos, and meats. Piedmonte is also home to the prized porcini mushroom, which is prevalent in many local dishes. A popular meal is *fonduta*, a melted cheese dip of milk, eggs, and the famous white truffles. *Bagna Cauda* is a raw vegetable fondue with hot anchovy dip and, of course, white truffles. Other regional favorites include game such as rabbit and boiled meat dishes like *Vitello Tonnato*, which is veal with tuna sauce. Piedmonte offers a multitude of high-quality cheeses, which include the flavorful Gorgonzola, Taleggio, Grana Padano, and Castelmagno, a time-honored cheese of exceptional quality produced in very small quantities.

Divine Wine: In terms of region and size, Piedmonte is Italy's largest DOC zone and home to seven of the country's twenty-five DOCG appellations. The light and fruit-forward white wines of Asti and Gavi are produced here, but the area is primarily known for the big, tannic reds of Barolo, Barbaresco, and Gattinara, with just enough of the lighter Barbera and Dolcetto to round out the offerings. Known as "the king of wines, the wine of kings," Barolo is arguably Italy's greatest red wine. It is produced from 100 percent Nebbiolo grapes grown on the hills around the town of Barolo and is aged in oak or chestnut casks for a minimum of three years, which contributes to its smoky flavor. In this DOCG, wine that has aged a minimum of five years in the cask can be labeled "Riserva." Barolo's younger cousin, Barbaresco, is also made from 100 percent Nebbiolo grapes, but from an area about twenty-five miles northeast of Barolo. Typically lighter in style, it is only aged two years, one year of which is in casks. Both are capable of matching up to hearty pastas, stews, red meats, game, and

OPPOSITE: One of the most enchanting discoveries on the Italian Riviera is the small fishing village of Camogli, nestled between the Ligurian Sea and Portofino Mountain. Hotel Cenobio Dei Dogi is shown at the far right end. THIS PAGE: The terraced suites of Royal Hotel Sanremo give way to bondless views of the Mediterranean Sea along the Italian Riviera.

Gorzonzola cheese. Hints of violets, chocolate, and prunes are typical of both. Gattinara is a small DOCG zone in Northwestern Italy, between and just north of the area between Turin and Milan. These red wines are typically 90 percent Nebbiolo grapes with the balance, Bonarda. Full bodied and elegant, with hints of violets and spices, some of these wines can easily age for ten to fifteen years. Barbera is Italy's most planted grape, and is straightforward and easy-drinking. Red fruit aromas dominate this light-bodied wine, proving the belief that wine is meant to be consumed with meals and without a lot of bother. Most will be labeled with the name of the village of production (e.g. Barbera d'Asti, Barbera d'Alba, etc.). If it is simply labeled "Barbera" it can be from anywhere. This wine goes well with tomato-based sauces, pizza, and antipasto. Dolcetto is Piedmonte's second most widely planted grape. Its name means "the little sweet one" and thus should be consumed young and relatively cool—not warmer than sixty degrees Fahrenheit. The wine is, however, dry, low in acidity, and highly tannic, making it a good match for poultry and most meat dishes. Gavi, is made from the Cortese grape, primarily grown in a dozen or so small villages just north of Genoa. These sensational white wines (Arneis, in particular, is very worth trying) are superb with seafood, fish dishes, and white meats. Once nearly extinct, the Cortese grape has made a comeback in the area north of the town of Alba. It produces exceptional wines with characteristics of apples, pears, and a hint of licorice – wonderful on their own and also with fish.

Liguria

Liguria is a narrow strip of land, encircled by the Mediterranean Sea, the Maritime Alps, and the Apennines mountains. Its flora and fauna are among the most diverse and interesting in Italy. Liguria's natural, rich beauty has inspired an array of endearing names such as "Paradise Gulf," "Siren Bay," "Bay of Silence," "Bay of Fairy Tales," and "Sea's Echo." The coastline is geographically divided between the Western Riviera and the Eastern Riviera. Serving as the region's capital and center point, the city of Genoa divides the region into the *Riviera di Ponente*, which extends west to the French border and is characterized by long sand and pebble beaches, and the *Riviera di Levante*. This beautiful stretch of coastline begins with smooth, sandy beaches, climbs magnificently precipitous jagged cliffs, and then rolls into the peaks of the Appennines. Sanremo is the crown jewel of the *Riviera di Ponente* and one of the most esteemed spots of Liguria. The city is Italy's flower capital and owes its fame primarily to the *Festival della Canzone* (Italian music competition). Nonetheless, its glamorous

OPPOSITE: Sip a cappuccino and enjoy the sunrise as you slowly make your way through the endless assortment of fresh breakfast fare typical of most Luxury Family Hotel & Resorts. Shown here: Hotel Cenobio Dei Dogi, Camogli. THIS PAGE: The Grand Visconti Palace is the only Luxury Resort in Milan. Here, you'll discover the joys of calmly relaxing in a gracious environment after a day touring this remarkable capital of Lombardy.

boutiques and ancient village are not to be underestimated. The *Riviera di Levante* boasts cities whose names are internationally renowned. The Tigullio Gulf includes Rapallo, Sestri, Portofino, and Camogli, which perhaps remains the most authentic of the towns. Further south sits the breathtaking charm of the Cinque Terre, five small towns each with their own particular allure, perched along the coast's cliffs. At the end of the Riviera is the *Golfo dei Poeti* (Poets Gulf), which includes the towns of Lerici and Portovenere.

Classic Cuisine: The basis of all recipes is olive oil, and the most well-known is the basil *pesto* sauce, traditionally served as *trenette col pesto* with its main ingredients of fresh basil, pine nuts, olive oil, garlic, and Parmesan cheese. There are a wide variety of *ravioli*; the most typical is *pansotti con salsa di noci*, filled with Swiss chard, basil, Ricotta, and Parmesan cheese with a walnut sauce. Ligurian pies are perhaps the most flavorful, from the simple *focaccia* with oil and salt, to *torta pasqualina*, a savory Easter pie with layers of pastry filled with spinach, egg, herbs, ricotta, and *Parmigiano* cheese. Veal is one of the most commonly used meats and includes recipes such as *Cima ripiena alla Genovese*, which is stuffed breasts of veal with vegetables, herbs, pine nuts, and Parmesan cheese. But fish like cod, sardines, mullet, tuna, swordfish, sea bass, squid, and especially anchovies are the most revered on the Ligurian coast and are served in a variety of ways:

in soups and stews, as a *fritti misti* (mixed selection fried), or as a fish salad. Mussels are a popular dish, typically served as *zuppa di cozze* (mussel soup). Ligurians are fond of vegetables as well, particularly those that can be stuffed, like *fiori di zucchini ripieni* (Stuffed zucchini blossoms). Their desserts are simple and often fried, like *ravioli dolci* (sweet ravioli).

Divine Wine: This region produces a very small, but flavorful group of wines. Some of the most outstanding are the reds of Ormeasco (Dolcetto) origin, a grape produced in Ormea, located on the border between Liguria and Piedmonte.

THIS PAGE: Trentino-Alto Adige's Hotel Elephant's gourmet restaurant will captivate you with its traditional yet inventive style. OPPOSITE: Hotel Bellevue exudes a harmonic balance of rustic charm and sophisticated elegance; Chef Sergio Sesone prepares a variety of regional and international cuisine at the hotel's four award-winning eateries.

Lombardy

Nestled in the middle of Northern Italy, with the Swiss Alps forming part of its northernmost borders, Lombardy comprises the main section of the Po River Valley and is one of Italy's busiest commercial-industrial regions. As Lombardy's capital and its largest city, Milan is a modern, prosperous city, and hosts the Italian headquarters of many banks and corporations. It is also renowned, along with Paris and New York, as a major center of fashion and design. Blending the old and the new, Milan has many points of interest, including impressive cathedrals like the Duomo di Milano (locally referred to as Il Duomo), incredible designer shopping and boutiques, La Scala (a world-renowned opera house), Leonardo's *The Last Supper* in the church of Santa Maria delle Grazie, and the enchanting *Navigli* district, whose canals play host to the city's young crowd in numerous entertaining bars and restaurants. Lake Como is a favorite vacation spot for Europeans, thanks to its combination of fine art, gorgeous scenery, and invigorating mountain air. From here, you can take a relaxing boat trip to view the many noble villas and gardens, or venture to the charming villages of Bellagio, Tremezzo, and Varenna. Piazza Cavour, in the town of Lake Como, has lakeside cafes and fashionable shopping boutiques, as well as breathtaking views of the snow-capped Alps. Nearby is Lake Maggiore, with its three islands: Isola Bella, Isola dei Pescatori, and Isola Madre. Three other Lombardy towns deserving a visit are Bergamo, with its Piazza Vecchia, considered one of the most picturesque squares in all of Italy; Mantova's Ducal Palace, with its series of frescoes by Mantegna; and Cremona, home to the master artisan of stringed instruments, Stradivari. In line with the region's natural beauty and popularity of outdoor activities, golf courses in this region are considered some of Italy's most beautiful.

Classic Cuisine: Visitors will find Lombardy to be exceptionally diverse in the culinary realm. Each city has its own gastronomic history and style. Milan, in particular, seems to be a freethinking city, and consequently, more inclined to contemporary cuisine in which specialties from different Italian regions are merged with local dishes. Lombardy is known for its rice dishes, the most common being *Risotto alla Milanese*, which is a creamy saffron short-grain rice, blended with meat or chicken stock, onion, pepper and Parmesan cheese. One of the region's favorite pastas is pumpkin *tortelli* from Mantua, but the *Ossobuco* (stewed veal shank) still remains a traditional main course. Other distinctive ingredients include olive oil, freshly cured meats, and remarkable cheeses, such as the

richly flavored Gorgonzola, Crescenza, Grano Padano, Mascarpone (primarily used to make desserts and mousses), and Bito, which has been in existence since the start of the 11th century.

Divine Wine: Wine production in Lombardy is broken down into districts, each cultivating different grapes. Lugana is home to Valpolicella (red), Amarone (red), and Soave (white). Franciacorta is known for its production of sparkling wines made using traditional champagne methods, like *spumante*, as well as Cabernet and Merlot-based whites. Valetellina produces highly regarded wines based largely on a local version of Nebbiolo, the Piedmont noble grape known as Chiavannesca. Chardonnay, Pinot Bianco, Pinot Grigio, and Pinot Nero are produced around Breganze, a regional sub-district with its own DOC.

Trentino–Alto Adige

This area along Italy's northeastern border with Austria is a spectacular territory of jagged ridges and snow-capped peaks, sparkling waterfalls and sweeping meadows, fabulous ski resorts and enchanting medieval towns. In winter, the skiing is absolutely first rate. Spring and fall offer captivating hikes and climbs along a wide range of well-marked trails with stops in distant mountain hamlets. Castles abound, and many are open to visitors; some have even been transformed into hotels and restaurants. As the name suggests, Trentino–Alto Adige is split into two provinces:

Trentino in the south is mostly Italian speaking and includes the towns of Trento, Rovereto, Madonna di Campiglio, and Riva del Garda. Südtirol or South Tyrol, the northern area of Alto Adige, includes Bolzano, Bressanone, and Merano. Italy annexed South Tyrol in 1919; it was previously part of Austria-Hungary, hence the prevalence of German speakers. For lovers of culture and history, this area has much to offer with numerous historic sites, museums, and important monuments. The city of Bozen remains to this day predominantly German, and thus is a showcase for many aspects of that culture, including the South Tyrol Museum of Archaeology, where the five-thousand-year-old "Iceman," discovered in 1991, is housed. Brixen/Bressanone is the main town of the valley, which exudes artistic and historical riches and a special charm. The Plose Mountain soars over the town and is a prominent ski resort. Meran/Merano is famous for its parks, gardens, promenades, footpaths, and medieval town center. Trento/Trentino stands at the crossroads of Italian and Northern

THIS PAGE: The stunning Palazzo Barbarigo Sul Canal Grande hotel occupies a prime location in a neighborhood that provides some of Venice's best shopping. OPPOSITE: The elegant Ca' dei Frati is one of four outstanding restaurants at San Clemente Palace Hotel & Resort, Venice.

European cultures. Visit the Castello del Buonconsiglio, the castle that was home to the prince bishops of Trento for many centuries, as well as the *duomo* with its splendid square.

Classic Cuisine: Trentino–Alto Adige shares culinary traditions with both the Italian and German sides of its border. The staples are polenta (corn meal), prepared in various ways, along with wild fowl, river trout, sauerkraut, and smoked meat, particularly local *speck* (juniper-flavored prosciutto). A favorite dish throughout Trentino–Alto Adige, *canederli* are *gnocchi* (dumplings) made from bread and flour and served in a broth. Mushrooms are plentiful and are used to make thick, flavorful sauces served with polenta, pasta, and, most commonly, meat dishes. Vegetables used are primarily beets, cabbage, potatoes, and turnips. The region's apples are full of flavor, making traditional strudels irresistible. *Zelten,* a mixture of yeast, flour, milk, sugar, butter, walnuts, dried figs, sultanas (golden raisins), pine nuts, and candied fruit, was once eaten only at Christmas. As the symbolic dessert of the region, today it is sold year round in pastry shops. The region's most important cheese is Grana Trentino, although Grana Padano DOP and Asiago DOP may also be made in the province. Each Alpine village makes its own variety called *nostrano* (our own).

Divine Wine: The predominant wines of the region are divided into three groups: those of French origin (Chardonnay, Sauvignon, Cabernet Franc, Cabernet Sauvignon, Pinot Nero), German origin (Muller-Thurgau, Rhine Riesling, Sylvaner), and Italian or local origin (Pinot Bianco, Malvasia, Pinot Grigio, Moscato Giallo, Moscato Rosa, Schiava, and a few others). High-quality Gewürztraminers are also readily available. The area around Tenuta San Leonardo produces more New World types of wines familiar to Americans, including Cabernet and Merlot.

Veneto

This area is a hidden treasure and relatively unpopulated with tourists. Most people associate this region with Venice, a fascinating city of labyrinthine canals and alleyways, charming homes, notable villas, and impressive squares with stately buildings. The Jewish ghetto of Venice is an extraordinary and unique quarter with five synagogues (15th to 16th century) and ancient pawnshops. To venture no farther than Venice, however, would be to

miss so many other magnificent locales of this region. Verona, for instance, is one of Veneto's most eye-catching and historical cities. It is home to the Capulet house with Juliet's legendary balcony, outstanding Roman ruins, and magnificent examples of Medieval and Renaissance buildings. The city is full of music, and its piazzas and streets are especially festive during the annual summer opera festival held in the Roman Arena. Vicenza is an essential visit for any lover of architecture. Andrea Palladio moved here as a child and has, without a doubt, left his mark throughout the city. He is known for a fundamental use of column rows and a harmonization of his work in accordance with the surrounding land. In Padua, one can also appreciate works by Medieval and Renaissance artists, of whom Giotto's frescoes are perhaps the most important. Valpolicella is a fertile valley covered with innumerable family wineries that offer enchanting countryside and never-ending panoramas. Fifteenth-century walls surround Treviso, perfectly safeguarding its remarkable architectural and artistic masterpieces. Abano, a thermal spa town located in the center of this region, has hot water springs that have drawn visitors since Roman times. Chioggia, a mini-Venice with picturesque canals and busy riverbanks, is alive with people buying fish and vegetables in the markets. Bassano del Grappa is renowned for its centuries-old production of grappa and handcrafted ceramics, its Palladian covered wooden bridge, and wonderful shops. Lake Garda, surrounded by the Alps, is perfect for windsurfing, sailing, and canoeing, as well as for yachting and fishing. In Marostica, you can watch a human chess game whose pieces are dressed in Renaissance costume. The game has been played this way since 1454, when Marostica belonged to the Venetian Republic. Few places are more picturesque than Cortina d'Ampezzo, one of Europe's chicest ski resorts.

Classic Cuisine: The cuisine of Venice is traditionally herb-and-spice-based, a tradition that goes back to the days when the European spice trade was controlled from the city. The cuisine

THIS PAGE: Immerse yourself in the passionate art of Italian cooking at la cucina (the kitchen) of Villa Franceschi and Villa Margherita's restaurants. OPPOSITE: Whether you are a beginner just learning about wine or a seasoned oenophile, Villa Luppis's extensive wine cellar is the ideal space in which to experience the world of Italian wine. Friuli Venezia Giulia produces thirty varieties of grapes.

is mainly polenta (corn meal) and rice, along with assorted shellfish, fresh fish, wild fowl, and mushrooms. Typical courses include *risotto nero* (black squid risotto), *Fegato alla Veneziana* (pan-fried calf's liver) and radicchio, red chicory most often served grilled or as a salad. Venetian cooks masterfully combine various ingredients and create sauces that enhance original flavors. The unusual *Asparagi di Bassano* (white asparagus of Bassano), prepared in a variety of ways, is legendary. Italians have been making an incredible array of cured meats for thousands of years, and in the Veneto, pork with the addition of chicken liver or veal is most prevalent. Asiago DOC/DOP is the finest cheese, while tiramisu is the most renowned dessert of the region.

Divine Wine: The Veneto is also one of Italy's top regions in total wine production, known for producing full-bodied reds like Bardolino, Valpolicella, Cabernet Sauvignon, and Cabernet. The sparkling Prosecco is combined with peaches to create the refreshing Bellini, Veneto's signature drink made famous at Harry's Bar in the Cipriani Hotel in Venice. The original was made with Prosecco, puree of fresh white peaches, and raspberry garnish. The drink was so named because the resulting pink color matched almost exactly the color of a toga worn by a saint in a 15th-century Giovanni Bellini painting.

Friuli Venezia Giulia

Situated in Italy's northeastern corner, Friuli is close to Austria, Slovenia, and Croatia. Though not often mentioned in guidebooks, Friuli is a diverse region teeming with beaches, secluded alpine villages, Roman ruins, splendid country villas, snow-capped mountains, rocky seaside cliffs, seaports, and picturesque fishing villages. Trieste, the area's primary sightseeing destination, is home to the Cathedral of San Giusto, with two Romanesque basilicas that were united in the 14th century. If you are interested in archaeology, the arch of Riccardo (33 B.C.) and the Roman theatre (1st and 2nd centuries A.D.) are inspiring sites. Triste's Giuseppe Verdi theatre hosts its famed opera season, in addition to the International Operetta Festival. Extending out into the sea, the wonderfully preserved medieval Castle of Miramare features grounds with English and Italian gardens, unusual plants, sculptures, and ponds. In Gorizia, the esteemed Attems Petzenstein Palace houses an art museum and the Museum of the Synagogue. Along with documentation on the history of the Jewish community, paintings of the poet and philosopher Carlo Michelstaedter are on display. The Marano Lagoon is home to countless migrating waterfowl, while Grado is a village composed of narrow streets reminiscent of Venice's smaller canals and pathways. This ancient fishing village is adjacent to a beach resort and a well-known health spa.

Classic Cuisine: Polenta (corn meal) is the food most often found on a table in Friuli, and is often accompanied by flavorsome sauces, game, chicken, rabbit, or salted cheeses such as *frico*, fried in butter. Soups are typically made with beans, greens, or pork ribs, and a plentiful serving of lard. *Prosciutto di San Daniele* DOP is considered one of the world's best hams, made only by twenty-seven small producers within the town of San Daniele. The woodlands are abundant with mushrooms, herbs, fruit crops, and game. Trieste and Grado culinary styles are influenced by the Venetian manner of preparing seafood, with definitive Slavic and Austrian flavors. Typical favorites, especially around Trieste, are *Iota*, a bean, potato, and white cabbage soup; *Porcina*, a mix of boiled pork with sauerkraut, mustard, and horseradish; and a Slavic-style goulash and dumplings. Seafood, including turbot, sardines, prawns, cuttlefish, squid, scallops, crabs, and eels, is favored along the coastline. Montasio DOP cheese has been an export of the region since the 18th century, and can only be produced legally within Friuli Venezia-Giulia and certain Veneto provinces. Some typical desserts are German-style apple strudel and *crostoli*, a fried dough.

Divine Wine: Friuli produces thirty varieties of grapes and is to white wines in Italy what Piedmont and Tuscany are to reds. Their whites are classically restrained in tone, the epitome of refinement. The predominant white is the now world-famous Pinot Grigio, but other notable wines include Ribolla Gialla, Pinot Bianco, Riesling Italico, Moscato Giallo, and Chardonnay. Reds include the herbaceous Refosco dal Peduncolo Rosso and the spicy, fruity Schiappettino, also called Ribola Nera.

GRAND HOTEL SITEA

via Carlo Alberto 35 | 10123 Turin, Italy
Tel. + 39 0115170171 | Fax: + 39 011548090
E-mail: sitea@thi.it | Web site: www.sitea.thi.it

Exclusive Luxury Family Offer: DISCOVERING TURIN: Arrival Friday or Saturday, with accommodations that include 2 nights double room or deluxe double room based on availability; buffet breakfast; late check-out 6.00 p.m.; a convenient, self-guided tour kit; the Torino & Piedmonte Card, a comprehensive 48-hour museum and urban public transport pass; no charge for a child up to 12 years old on bed and breakfast basis sharing room with parents. Valid All Year with a minimum two nights stay for adults. Price from €145 per person; third bed €60. From third week in July through end of August, arrival any day price from €115 per person. Please reference at time of reservation: LFHR-09.

GRAND HOTEL SITEA sits in the heart of Turin, behind the Piazza San Carlo. A fixture in the life of Turin for three-quarters of the 20th century, the Sitea earned a well-known award in 2001: it was included in the listing of historic establishments of the Associazione Locali Storici d'Italia. The experienced management, most of whom have been part of the carefully selected staff for decades, and the elegant surroundings make the hotel indispensable to families seeking a luxury experience. As the city's Art Nouveau symbol of refined hospitality, the hotel is decorated in classic period style, with the suite and junior suites featuring exclusive furnishings, prints, and fabrics. Many of the individual rooms can be joined in order to accommodate larger families, and services abound to accommodate a variety of needs. One such thoughtful amenity is the "Personal Shopper," an accompanied tour of the city's trendy shops and charming boutiques. After a day spent shopping or touring the sights, the on-site bar offers a pleasant, relaxed atmosphere for a pre-dinner drink. Teatime is available October through April and includes a selection of oriental blends accompanied by petite delicacies and haute patisserie. With its stylish Empire-style decor, the Carignano restaurant offers sophisticated international cuisine with dishes crafted in the renowned Piedmontese tradition. Savor unique signature dishes such as Muscovy duck breasts with Martin Sec pears in red wine. The beautiful internal garden is ideal for romantic candlelit dinners or intimate family gatherings. The *Michelin Guide*, as well as other notable restaurant reviewers, gives Carignano excellent ratings. Turin and the Grand Hotel Sitea are the perfect hosts for family celebrations and other events; together they personify a refined embodiment of hospitality in this post–2006 Winter Olympics location.

FINE POINTS

Our Family Loved Most: Exceptional base from which to explore the best of Turin's important sights, historic walks, restaurants, and nightlife, only to return to a rare quality of service and attentiveness.

Rooms: 120 rooms, including suites and junior suites.

Food: Bar; Carignano restaurant.

Suggested ages for kids: All ages; no charge for a child up to 12 years old sharing room with parents.

Special Features: Sites within minutes of the hotel's front steps include: the Ancient History Museum, National History Museum of Artillery, Museum of the Holy Shroud, National Museum of Cinema, Botanical Gardens, and Rivoli Castle; personal shopping service; four conference rooms able to host up to 100 people.

GRAND VISCONTI PALACE

Viale Isonzo, 14 | 20135 Milan (Milano), Italy
Tel. +39 02540341 | Fax: +39 0254069523
E-mail: info@grandviscontipalace.com | Web site: www.grandviscontipalace.com

Exclusive Luxury Family Offer: Free entrance to the Grand Visconti Palace Health Club with use of pool, gym, and steam area; non-inclusive of massage or beauty treatments. Please reference at time of reservation: LFHR-09.

GRAND VISCONTI PALACE is a peaceful green oasis amid Italy's economic capital of Milan. The hotel is situated in a residential area just a few minutes away from Porta Romana, one of the ancient city gates, which marked the border of the center of old Milan. The park area is eye-catching, as is the classical Italian garden and English-style lawn, hedges of lavender, and fountains. Three Art Deco cast-iron gazebos house an open-air bar, tables, and relaxing sofas; one is used throughout the cooler season. Cane chaise lounges are situated among flower gardens that bloom into life each spring. The state-of-the-art full-service wellness center is a haven of tranquility after a full day touring the incredible sights and shops of this trendy Italian city. The lovely pool inside the center beckons guests through a large glass picture window, and leads to the Turkish bath, sauna, and Jacuzzi. Refined decorations, select Italian marble, and Murano crystal lamps and lights envelop guests in an atmosphere rich in warmth and elegance. All rooms are of a classical décor, and the suites embody the utmost in stylish sophistication. Our favorite is the exclusive Tower Suite, which comprises three floors connected by a winding staircase and private elevator. The cathedral-like views of Milan from the private, sunken Jacuzzi on the suite's rooftop are enchanting. The Visavis bar is the ideal place for before-dinner drinks and informal meetings in an intimate setting, and the Salone Visconti is available for banquets and functions. Restaurant "al V piano" serves Mediterranean cuisine plus all the great, classic Lombardy and Milanese dishes.

FINE POINTS

Our Family Loved Most: The experience of being in a refuge of calm in the midst of this grand city along with quality spa treatments.
Rooms: 162 classic rooms; 10 suites, ranging from junior to the 3-level Tower Suite.
Food: Visavis bar; "al V piano" restaurant.
Suggested Ages for Kids: 8 and up.
Special Features: Classical Italian gardens; "Not Just Jazz," an intimate Milanese music club; full-service wellness center; indoor pool; Turkish bath; sauna; Jacuzzi.

HOTEL ANCORA

Corso Italia, 62, 32043 | Cortina d'Ampezzo (Belluno) Italy

Tel. +39 04363261 | Fax: +39 04363265

E-mail: info@hotelancoracortina.com | Web site: www.hotelancoracortina.it

Exclusive Luxury Family Offer: Fruit basket in room upon arrival. Please reference at time of reservation: LFHR-09.

HOTEL ANCORA is located on the pedestrian mall that encircles the center of Cortina, one of the world's most famous resort towns. Nestled in a lush valley beneath the Dolomite Alps, Cortina has long attracted everyone from rugged Alpine enthusiasts to the international jet set. This award-winning hotel has been a *Veneto Region*'s Quality Hotel every year since 1997, and in 2006 was chosen by *Gambero Rosso* as one of Italy's eleven best hotels. Built in 1826 in the *Ampezzano* style with wooden balconies and intricately carved and painted detailing, the hotel is not only beautiful but also famously accommodating. Owners Flavia and Renato Sartor delight in taking a personal interest in their guests' comfort. Once, we saw Flavia loan her mink coat to a guest who hadn't packed warmly enough. While the rooms are extremely posh and decorated with the finest antiques, they are also comfortable. The suites and junior suites have flower-laden balconies facing Cortina's main promenade, a great place to sit, relax, and people watch. In the winter, the town buzzes with the excitement of being one of Europe's top skiing destinations. In the summer, it's a top spot for biking and climbing. Legendary shopping opportunities are of course available year round. If you have an artistic interest, Hotel Ancora sponsors a salon hosted by the well-known writer Milena Milani and offers exhibitions by illustrious painters, sculptors, and other artists as well as conferences and cultural debates. The main dining room casts a spell with candlelit tables, classical music, gothic arches, and international cuisine perfectly prepared and presented. The Viennese Terrace cafe, decorated in Biedermeier style, overlooks the promenade, and the more informal Artist's Tavern is open for late-night dining. All restaurants offer the very best in Italian wines.

FINE POINTS

Our Family Loved Most: Joining Flavia and other guests on a private skiing excursion Flavia had designed especially for us, and which included being pulled on skies by horses!
Rooms: 56 rooms, including suites and junior suites.
Food: Artist's Tavern; Viennese Terrace café; Hotel Ancora, an outstanding, award-winning restaurant, whose chef won second prize in the World Cooking Competition in 2006 and a silver medal in the same competition in 2007.
Suggested Age for Kids: All ages.
Special Features: Each room proudly displays its Touring Club guide certificate for "Stanze Italiane," honoring Hotel Ancora's dedication to authentic and historic style for the years 2005 through 2008; suites and junior suites with balconies on Cortina's main promenade, hydrotherapy tubs, and Jacuzzi showers; fitness facility; sauna; spa; Wi-Fi and Internet connection; dry cleaning; non-smoking rooms; pets allowed; room service; artistic and literary salon, conferences, and debates; free shuttle bus transport to the slopes.

Gruppo Guide Alpine

Scuola di Alpinismo | Corso Italia 69/a "Ciasa de ra Regoles" | 1-32043 Cortina d'Ampezzo (BL), Italy

Tel./Fax: +39 0436868505

E-mail: info@guidecortina.com | Web site: www.guidecortina.com

Exclusive Luxury Family Offer: Ten percent discount on all programmed activities such as snow-shoeing, back country skiing courses, vie ferrate, climbing courses, and trekking (group excursions). No discount for private guides. Please reference at time of reservation: LFHR-09.

GRUPPO GUIDE ALPINE CORTINA have been leading trips through the Dolomites as far back as the early 1400s, when the Venetian Republic hired local trekkers to map out an official route along the Austrian-Venetian border. Eventually, those guides led pleasure trips as well, gaining such renown for their skill that, in 1865, the Austrian state officially authorized the discipline of Alpine Guide. Today, the twenty-eight UIAGM-certified guides of Gruppo Guide Alpine Cortina proudly carry on that Alpine tradition. With more than a hundred years of experience and knowledge in the Dolomites and surrounding mountains, the company specializes in custom climbing, mountaineering, and related mountain sports adventures for children and adults of every age. With fun in mind and safety a top priority at all times, the guides excel in matching the right trip to the right group to ensure everyone an unforgettable mountain adventure. They also offer an outstanding children's program, based on the belief that exposure to mountain activities at a young age helps develop equilibrium, coordination, and respect for the outdoors. Individual and group trips are available year round and include hiking, orienteering, climbing, back country skiing, snowshoeing, ice climbing, and trekking excursions. Custom trips can be crafted to match any level of experience and interest. Recently, our Adventure Sports Travel Specialist Isaac Levinson joined the company's seasoned guide Davide Alberti on an exhilarating off-piste skiing adventure. Not only was Isaac impressed with Davide's skill in navigating the ungroomed trails, but also in his incredible attention to the details necessary to ensure a fun and safe experience. Whether your family wants to learn the basics of climbing, hike a local scenic route, or test its skill along unmarked slopes, Gruppo Guide Alpine Cortina will make your dream adventure a reality.

Summer activities: Vie ferrate ascents, rock climbing, climbing school, hiking, Nordic walking.
Winter activities: In- and off-piste skiing, back country skiing, snowshoeing, ice climbing.

HOTEL BELLEVUE

Rue Grand Paradis, 22 | 11012 Cogne (Vallée d'Aoste), Italy
Tel. +39 016574825 | Fax: +39 0165749192
E-mail: info@hotelbellevue.it | Web site: www.hotelbellevue.it

Exclusive Luxury Family Offer: Free access to Valheureusa Wellness Oasis and free Hay Bath treatment included in room price. Please reference at time of reservation: LFHR-09.

HOTEL BELLEVUE is located in Val d'Aosta, one of the most splendid and picturesque regions of Italy, bordering both Switzerland and France. It is surrounded by breathtaking views of the Prateria dell'Orso and is opposite a glacier in the heart of the Gran Paradiso national park in the center of Cogne. Hotel Bellevue continues to be lovingly run by the Jeantet Roullet family, who has welcomed guests to this delightful property for four generations. A harmonic balance of rustic charm and sophisticated elegance was achieved through the careful renovation of this ancient alpine lodge, which still conveys its historical and antique atmosphere. This is just the right place for a family getaway year round, especially for nature enthusiasts and lovers of outdoor sports such as cross-country skiing, walking, and ice climbing, which are abundant throughout the area. Voted best spa of 2006 by Relais & Chateaux, the La Valheureusa Wellness Oasis provides luxury spa and beauty treatments like "Thermal Cave of the Hot Stone," the King Victor's bath with water aromatized by local wine, herbs, spices and honey, and the milk- and honey-based Cleopatra's Bath. High-end skin care products are also available. Under the superb artistic talent of Chef Sergio Sesone, four award-winning eateries offer guests a variety of regional and international cuisine: the Gourmet dell'Hotel Bellevue (which are reserved for families with children); the Bar à Fromage, Le Petite Restaurant, and le Brasserie du Bon Bec, which is located in Cogne's main square, just one hundred meters from the hotel. All feature vegetables, fruits, and herbs grown at the hotel's on-site organic garden. Once a week during the summer, a barbecue is organized in the on-site mountain hut, which is a very special experience.

FINE POINTS

Our Family Loved Most: The luxury atmosphere and amenities located within such beautiful natural surroundings give off an aura of romance and exclusivity, while also being family-friendly.
Rooms: 28 rooms plus 7 suites with Jacuzzi's, fireplaces, and some with private saunas; 3 chalets with fireplaces.
Food: Terrazzo (lunchtime a la carte); Gourmet dell'Hotel Bellevue; Bar a Fromage; Brasserie du Bon Bec; Le Petite Restaurant; cheese cellar; wine cellar with over 1,000 vintages.
Suggested Ages for Kids: All ages.
Special Features: La Valheureusa Wellness Oasis; summer excursions include free climbing, mountaineering, mountain biking, fishing, tennis, mini-golf, alpine guides, and weekly barbecue in mountain hut; winter excursions include cross-country skiing, alpine skiing, snow walks, snow rackets, ice falls, ski mountaineering, and le Vallée Blanche ski school; yearround excursions include horseback riding, nature guides, museums, castles, parks, waterfalls, lace production, cable crossing of Mount Blanc, panoramic flights, and a trek along the 56-meter-high, 50-meter-long Pondel Roman bridge.

RISTORANTE BAITA ERMITAGE

Località Ermitage | Courmayeur (AO) - 11013
Tel. +39 0165844351

> Ristorante Baita Ermitage is located in Courmayeur, a city long regarded as the culinary showcase of the Val d'Aosta. With its proximity to both Switzerland and France, a decidedly independent culinary spirit infuses this region's cuisine.

In keeping with that spirit, Baita Ermitage uses many French and Alpine ingredients to create flavorful, downhome dishes designed for maximum sustenance in the mountainous climate as well as elegant, sophisticated creations that delight as well as nourish. One delicacy not to be missed is *zuppa di pane*, a slow-baked bread and cheese soup made with bread, Fontina cheese, butter, and chicken stock. *Zuppa di Valpelline* raises the bar on traditional cabbage soup with the addition of fatty bacon and rosemary. Other Baita Ermitage dishes include cheese polenta, beef stew, and rabbit stew made with carrots, celery, onions, and spices. Variations of this dish often incorporate pheasant or marmot, which is marinated for two days in white wine to tenderize and flavor the meat. We stumbled upon Baita Ermitage one day while exploring the town. Although the small, charming dining room was full, outside the restaurant there are ample lounge chairs so we could dine in the midst of the fresh snow while enjoying both the exquisite cuisine and Alpine view. There, we had one of the best meals of our trip. The polenta especially was fantastic, prompting everyone in our family to order seconds, its rich flavor warming our bodies and delighting our taste buds as we enjoyed our meal, contentedly bundled up in our hats and coats. Whether for lunch or dinner, a meal at Ristorante Baita Ermitage is an experience in one of the world's great culinary styles—at once richly satisfying and yet with flavors delicately balanced to compare with the best cooking anywhere in Italy.

HOTEL CENOBIO DEI DOGI

Hotel Cenobio Dei Dogi | Via Cuneo, 34 | 16032 Camogli - Portofino Coast | Italy
Tel. +39 01857241 | Fax +39 0185772796
E-mail: reception@cenobio.it | Web site: www.cenobio.com | Member of: www.abitarelastoria.it

Exclusive Luxury Family Offer: 15 percent exchange rate discount for American citizens. Please reference at time of reservation: LFHR-09.

CENOBIO DEI DOGI grandly sits on a crest of rock above the Mediterranean Sea at the foot of Mount Portofino, just a short stroll from the old fishing village of Camogli. We're delighted to share this gem, which lies in such close proximity to the Cinque Terre, Portofino, and Santa Margherita Ligure, and is reminiscent of the time when few people knew of their magical allure. The hotel is surrounded by a lush park bordering the characteristically colored houses of the eastern Ligurian Riviera. Over four centuries ago Genoese Doges discovered this tranquil corner of what has been fittingly named "Paradise Gulf." Inspired by its peace and beauty, the Doges decided to claim this spot as their retreat, or *cenobio*. A 16th-century chapel dedicated to St. Emilio is still open to guests. The villa was passed down through generations of heirs, then purchased by the De Ferrari family, who in 1956 transformed it into a hotel. Antiques, Oriental rugs, and Etruscan artifacts adorn the hotel. Cenobio Dei Dogi's guest rooms and suites are simply furnished, offering either sea or garden views; we suggest one of the rooms with extensive balconies and striking vistas of Camogli's fishing port. Delight in the seawater swimming pool on the panoramic terrace with lounge-side service. Full service is also available at the private beach, which assures an uncommon luxuriousness among this popular area. Typical Ligurian dishes and seafood are featured at the Dei Dogi Restaurant, while wonderful seasonal specialties can be savored during the summer at La Playa. Cenobio's cuisine prevails on its own, but combine the exceptional food with the seaside location of both restaurants, waves pounding the shoreline, exceptional wine, and top-notch service, and the total experience reigns supreme.

FINE POINTS

Our Family Loved Most: Impeccable views of the sea coupled with unspoiled surroundings away from the touristy crowds.
Rooms: 105 rooms; 4 suites.
Food: Traditional Ligurian dishes and seafood are featured at the Dogi Restaurant, while delightful seasonal specialties can be savored in the summer at the La Playa seaside restaurant.
Suggested Ages for Kids: All ages.
Special Features: Swimming pool; tennis court; paddle trips along the coastal inlets; snorkeling; diving tours guided by local experts; meters from train for independent excursions to neighboring towns of the Italian Riviera; 7 meeting rooms for groups of 10 to 200 people, many with sea view and all with natural light and modern technical equipment and services.

HOTEL ELEPHANT

I-39042 Bressanone | Via Rio Bianco 4, South Tyrol, Italy
Tel. +39 0472832750 | Fax: +39 047283657
E-mail: info@hotelelephant.com | Web site: www.hotelelephant.com

Exclusive Luxury Family Offer: 5 NIGHTS IN A COMFORT ROOM: Fruit in room upon arrival; buffet breakfast daily; free entrance to steam bath and sauna; one visit to the house museum, "Elephant"; tour of the Novacella Abbey of the Augustinian Canons; one visit to the Pharmacy Museum. All reservations are on request and based upon availability. Price: from €400 per person. Please reference at time of reservation: LFHR-09.

HOTEL ELEPHANT is located in the charming town of Bressanone, also called Brixen, approximately forty kilometers north of Bolzano and forty-five kilometers south of the Brenner Pass dividing Italy and Austria. In 1550, King John of Portugal decided to give a unique gift to the Emperor Ferdinand of Austria, so he purchased an elephant in India, shipped it to Genoa, and then intended to walk it to Austria. The elephant tired as it neared Bressanone and was stabled for two weeks at the Am Hohen Feld Inn. Spectators came from all over to see the gigantic creature. Recognizing this as a great promotional opportunity, the inn's proprietor not only commissioned a large fresco of his biggest guest to be painted on the street wall, he also renamed the establishment Hotel Elephant. The tale continues to this day as does the inn with its splendid fresco. The present owners, the Heiss Family, are direct descendants of the Am Hohen Feld Inn proprietor. Today, Hotel Elephant continues to be a superb place for a family journey amid a pleasant atmosphere of personalized service and genuine hospitality. The hotel is appointed with fine museum-quality paintings, antiques, and attractive decor, intermingled with modern comforts. The beautifully landscaped park contains a swimming pool along with tennis courts, rose and trellised fruit gardens, and decorative fountains. The guestrooms are spacious and open onto balconies from which guests can enjoy incredible panoramic views of the Brixner Becken basin. The cuisine is exceptional as is the cozy ambience of the three dining rooms: the Altdeutsche Stube, the Apostelstube, and the Zirbelstube. Chef Viktor Grunser creates tantalizing menus highlighting unsurpassed regional dishes with Mediterranean accents.

FINE POINTS

Our Family Loved Most: The hotel's exquisite position in the charming town of Bressanone, surrounded by breathtaking Alpine scenery.
Rooms: 44 rooms to include single, deluxe, and junior suites.
Food: 3 dining rooms serving exceptional regional specialties: the Altdeutsche Stube, the Apostelstube, and the Zirbelstube.
Suggested Ages for Kids: All ages.
Special Features: Swimming pool with sunbathing terrace and patio bar; fitness center equipped with sauna, gym, and solarium; Wi-Fi Internet; park with gardens; meeting rooms for events of up to 65 people; wine and cultural tours upon request; minutes by foot to shops, boutiques, and cafés; close proximity to mountain biking, cycling along the Eisackdamm, horseback riding, hiking, tennis, paragliding, fishing, tobogganing, climbing for adults and children with expert mountain guides, rafting, kayaking, ice skating, skiing, and snowboarding.

HOTEL PORTOFINO KULM

Viale Bernardo Gaggini, 23 | Portofino Vetta - 16030 Ruta di Camogli, Italy

Tel. +39 01857361 | Fax: +39 0185776622

E-mail: kulm@portofinokulm.it | Web site: www.portofinokulm.it | Member of: www.abitarelastoria.it

Exclusive Luxury Family Offer: 15 percent exchange rate discount for American citizens. Please reference at time of reservation: LFHR-09.

HOTEL PORTOFINO KULM majestically sits on a mountaintop surrounded by inspiring views of two gulfs: the Tigullio to the east and the Paradise to the west, along with vistas of the Appenine Mountain ranges. In 1903 the founder, Sebastiano Gaggini, passionate about the refined way of life in Paris, set out to re-create an enhanced version of the Parisian lifestyle in this unique location on the Ligurian promontory. The hotel became a favorite of the Queen Mother Margherita and her entourage, as well as with other nobility, heads of state, Italian and foreign ministers, illustrious artists, scientists, and cultural leaders. Today, the hotel offers pleasant guest rooms with absolutely outstanding views facing the sea or the park. Portofino Kulm remains an ideal holiday spot for lovers of peace and nature. Located in the park of Mount Portofino, hikers can take advantage of the opportunity to explore the wonders of one of Italy's most beautiful nature reserves with its network of paths and trails for quiet walks as well as more strenuous hikes along its hills and valleys. Taking a swim in the indoor pool overlooking the garden, indulging in a luxurious spa treatment, or simply reading a book can turn even a short stay into a memorable experience. For lovers of the sea, a private beach is available at the nearby Hotel Cenobio Dei Dogi and is reachable by the hotel's shuttle. An elegant atmosphere with cuisine like no other awaits you at the Zeffirino Kulm restaurant. The Zeffirino family has been awarded the "Ambassador of Italian Cuisine in the World" for over four generations, and has captivated celebrities worldwide including Pavarotti, Pope John Paul II, and Frank Sinatra.

FINE POINTS

Our Family Loved Most: Outstanding views and cuisine in combination with tranquil setting that nonetheless remains close to Genoa, the characteristic fishing villages of Camogli, the Cinque Terre, and the exclusive marinas of Portofino, Santa Margherita Ligure, and Rapallo.
Rooms: 77 rooms, each with views of the sea or the park.
Food: Zeffirino Kulm restaurant, run by the Zeffirino family, acclaimed restaurateurs for four generations and famous for spreading Italian culinary art throughout the world.
Suggested Ages for Kids: All ages.
Special Features: Indoor swimming pool; fitness center and spa; tennis; mini-soccer courts; bar; reading lounge; hiking trails to well-known town of Santa Margherita Liguria and beyond; the Kursaal hall, located in a separate building, seats up to 350 people; together, the Portofino Kulm and nearby Hotel Cenobio Dei Dogi offer 184 guest rooms and a variety of meeting rooms.

HOTEL VILLA AMINTA

Via Sempione Nord | 123 28838 Stresa (Verbania) Italy
Tel. +39 0323933818 | Fax +39 0323933955
E-mail: villa-aminta@villa-aminta.it | Web site: www.villa-aminta.it

Exclusive Luxury Family Offer: Freshly baked Villa Aminta cookies in your room on arrival. Please reference at time of reservation: LFHR-09.

HOTEL VILLA AMINTA rises like a peaceful haven facing Lake Maggiore between the towns of Stresa and Baveno, overlooking the Borromeo Gulf and beautiful islands of Isola Bella, Isola Madre, and Isola dei Pescatori. Villa Aminta, once an elegant private residence, has been transformed into a five-star luxury hotel by the Zanetta family, the owners since 2000. They have brought the villa back to its original splendor, combining a fairy-tale feel with elegance, taste, and the highest standards of amenities and service. This 19th-century family villa has been carefully restored, and is embellished with antique furniture, stuccos, chandeliers, precious wallpapers, arabesques, and Oriental arches. The hotel rooms of Villa Aminta are very romantic, all featuring Italian furnishings, many with Murano lamps or chandeliers along with handmade frescoes. They range from midsize to spacious, each one tastefully and comfortably decorated. All open onto balconies or terraces with garden or lake views. The suites and junior suites have wonderful lakefront views from the balconies, all personalized and located on the top fourth floor. The luxurious Palazzo Aminta Beauty & Spa offers exclusive and personalized programs to rebalance the body and soul. Professor Nicola Sorrentino, a specialist much sought after by world-famous celebrities, coordinates the efforts of the experienced staff. Escape into their Zen meditation room for the deepest level of relaxation or indulge in a host of other healthful and beautifying services. Leisure activities abound, including special boat excursions leaving from the hotel docks for an unforgettable visit to the Borromeo Islands. Restaurant Le Isole, which overlooks beautiful Lake Maggiore, and Restaurant I Mori both serve delicious local and international dishes with a high-quality wine list for discerning palates.

FINE POINTS

Our Family Loved Most: Magnificent panoramic views of Borromeo Islands.
Rooms: 58 rooms; 5 suites; 5 junior suites.
Food: Restaurant à la carte; I Mori; Le Isole.
Suggested Ages for Kids: All ages.
Special Features: Special events and ceremonies; meeting room to accommodate from 10 to 100 persons; multilingual reception and concierge; outdoor swimming pool; private beach; tennis court; 3 boat moorings; limousine and helicopter services; private shuttle to and from Stresa; 24-hour room service; baggage and garage service; waterskiing; parachute; jet ski; natural park; Palazzo Aminta Beauty & Spa, offering treatments designed for new mothers, four-handed massage with essential hot oils, seaweed therapies or thermal mud bath, exfoliating, hydrating, and revitalizing face and body treatments, and more; fitness area; cooking lessons; cocktail-making lessons; wine tasting.

HOTEL VILLA CA' SETTE

Via Cunizza da Romano, 4, 36061 | Bassano del Grappa | Venice, Italy
Tel. +39 0424383350 | Fax: + 39 0424393287
E-mail: info@ca-sette.it | Web site: www.ca-sette.it

Exclusive Luxury Family Offer: Fruit basket and English newspaper in room upon arrival. Please reference at time of reservation: LFHR-09.

HOTEL VILLA CA' SETTE is situated near the medieval walled city of Bassano del Grappa about an hour northwest of Venice. With buildings that date as far back as the early 1500s, it thrived for centuries as a private estate. In 1994, the Zonta family foresaw a renewed purpose for the property and embarked on an imaginative restoration that blends Old World traditions with sleek, modern-day design. Beautiful, spacious rooms with full amenities are available in the property's three main buildings: the Villa, the Casa Colonica, and the Barchessa. The most outstanding family accommodation is the villa's two-bedroom Napoleon suite with its grand living room and frescoed ceilings. It can be interconnected with the two adjacent double rooms to make a four-bedroom, three-bath suite. A stay at Ca' Sette also means proximity to the charming town of Bassano del Grappa. Situated at the foot of Mount Grappa, it is a living slice of Italy's past. You can spend days exploring its streets, scenic piazzas, Gothic churches, and Andrea Palladio's famous bridge and have few encounters with throngs of tourists— only friendly Italian voices and enthusiastic gestures welcoming you into their shops and restaurants. A wealth of activities and festivals take place year round here, but the city is perhaps best known for its Asparagus Festival, a time each May when local restaurants celebrate the harvest with dishes featuring the region's famous white variety. Ca' Sette's Ristorante Ca' 7 is another treasure. The Zonta family also produces sought-after wines and olive oils, and these ingredients are used to perfection in a variety of dishes, along with fresh seasonal vegetables, local meats, and line-caught seafood. The two-hundred-bottle wine list also includes the owners' exceptional Cabernet Due Santi and Zonta reds.

FINE POINTS

Our Family Loved Most: Taking the private stairway from the Napoleon suite directly into the restaurant. Very exclusive!
Rooms: 19 rooms.
Food: Room service; restaurant serving breakfast, lunch, and dinner, closed on Sunday for dinner and Monday for lunch and dinner.
Suggested Age for Kids: All ages; until 8 years old free in parents' room.
Special Features: 24-hour reception; ample covered parking; Internet modem link and Wi-Fi; accommodations for business meetings and conferences with a wide range of audio-visual equipment on request; wedding and special events planning; bicycle rentals; summer-long outdoor concerts, cinema, and plays in Bassano del Grappa's plazas; hang-gliding, parasailing, and mountain bike competitions; hiking, biking, kayaking, ballooning, canoeing, and river rafting nearby.

HOTEL VILLA FRANCESCHI

Via Don Minzoni, 28 | Mira Porte (Venice) 30034, Italy
Tel. +39 0414266531 | Fax: +39 0415608996
E-mail: info@villafranceschi.com | Web site: www.villafranceschi.com

Exclusive Luxury Family Offer: Children up to 10 years old stay for free in all rooms. Please reference at time of reservation: LFHR-09.

VILLA FRANCESCHI is owned and operated by brothers Alessandro and Dario Dal Corso, whose family name is synonymous with refined hospitality. Like its sister hotel, Villa Margherita, the 16th-century Villa Franceschi is located in Mira Porte, right on the Brenta River, which is considered an extension of the Grand Canal. One of a string of 15th- and 16th-century villas built along the Brenta by the noble families of Venice, Villa Franceschi displays all the elements of a Venetian style home, with one façade facing the river, the other the spacious park out back with its beautiful gardens and antique statuary. Thus, almost all the rooms, whether in the villa itself or its adjacent Barchessa (the original servants' quarters), feature one of these two views. Many of the ground-floor rooms have their own independent entries right into the gardens as well. In its entirety, the hotel exudes an old-world elegance underlain with the best in modern-day amenities. Rooms are spacious and decorated with antique tapestries, linens, period furniture, and Murano glass chandeliers. Public rooms like the reception hall, sitting room, and the bar/lounge are the epitome of stylish elegance and comfort. Although one can easily spend days on-site exploring the natural and manmade beauty of this property, it also makes the perfect home base from which to explore the Brenta and its other villas, and Venice is only about thirty minutes away by bus or ferry. Inside the Barchessa is the on-site restaurant, La Veranda, a sun-drenched, spacious dining room from which guests enjoy a bountiful breakfast each morning. For a truly memorable experience in fine Venetian dining, the esteemed Ristorante Margherita located in the elegant 16th-century building of Villa Palladiana is not to be missed.

FINE POINTS

Our Family Loved Most: Breakfast out in the gardens among all its lovely greenery and blooming flowers.
Rooms: 8 deluxe rooms; 10 junior suites; 6 full suites.
Food: Bar/lounge; La Veranda restaurant; Ristorante Margherita.
Suggested Ages for Kids: All ages.
Special Features: Free breakfast; 24-hour front desk; babysitting/childcare services available; laundry service; private jogging track; fitness center/health club; swimming pool; hairdresser; golf and waterskiing nearby; meeting and banquet with business service and fax machine; pets welcome; complimentary transport to and from airport; nearby bus and ferry service to Venice; car rental.

HOTEL VILLA MARGHERITA

Via Nazionale, 416 | 30300 Mira Porte (Venice), Italy
Tel. +39 0414265800 | Fax +39 0414265838
E-mail: info@villa-margherita.com | Web site: www.villa-margherita.com

Exclusive Luxury Family Offer: Children up to 10 years old stay for free in all room categories. Please reference at time of reservation: LFHR-09.

HOTEL VILLA MARGHERITA is located just outside Mira Porte, on a scenic bend of the Brenta River twenty-five kilometers southwest of Venice. The history and romance inherent in this 16th-century Palladian-style villa is apparent from the start, with an approach that begins along a tree-dappled gravel avenue lined with antique statues and gives way to the elegant façade and arched portico of a building that epitomizes traditional Venetian elegance. This, and its sister hotel, Villa Franceschi, are hands down our favorite spots to stay when visiting Venice. Owned by the Dal Corso family, the hotel is run by brothers Alessandro and Dario who pay homage to its tradition of refined hospitality and comfort, while offering every amenity expected from a first-class, modern facility. Inside, nothing less than the finest antiques, tapestries, and linens embellish the guest rooms. The parlors and drawing rooms, with their elegant frescoes and welcoming fireplaces, exude harmony and tranquility. Outside, the arched portico encourages moments of relaxation and companionship, while the *campiello* opens onto the vista of an immense swath of greenery that comprises the parks behind the villa. Together, these private and communal spaces combine to form a relaxing and gracious retreat after a day spent wandering the crowded canals of Venice. One of the hotel's most delightful features, the family-run Ristorante Margherita, serves up authentic Venetian cuisine, an extensive wine list, and service that makes you feel like part of the family. Even if you haven't visited in several years, they somehow manage to remember your preferences. During our last visit, we were greeted with "Do you still prefer to begin with Louis Roederer Cristal 1994 along with carpaccio of salmon and scampi?" as though we'd just been in the night before.

FINE POINTS

Our Family Loved Most: The exceptional service, warmth, and thoughtfulness of the staff that reveals itself in even the smallest of details, like the luxuriously monogrammed bathrobes and bedroom slippers provided for each guest.
Rooms: 19 rooms.
Food: Bar/lounge; breakfast buffet; lunch and dinner at on-site Ristorante Margherita.
Suggested Ages for Kids: All ages.
Special Features: Fresh fruit basket upon arrival; 24-hour room service; babysitting/childcare services available; laundry service; cooking courses; wine tastings; bicycle rentals; private jogging track; tennis courts; fitness center/health club; hairdresser; golf and waterskiing nearby; pets welcome; conference and meeting rooms with business service and fax machine; complimentary transport to and from airport; nearby bus and ferry service to Venice.

LOCANDA DEI MAI INTEES

via Nobile Claudio Riva, 2 | 21022 Azzate (VA) | Italy

Tel. +39 0332457223 | Fax: +39 0332459339

E-mail: maiintees@tin.it | info@mai-intees.com | Web site: www.mai-intees.com | Member of: www.abitarelastoria.it

Exclusive Luxury Family Offer: LAKE REGION ROMANCE: With a minimum stay of 3 nights, one complimentary dinner for two. Please reference at time of reservation: LFHR-09.

LOCANDA DEI MAI INTEES lies in the heart of the Lake area with close proximity to Lake Maggiore, Lake Varese, and Lake Como. It is situated in the picturesque medieval town of Azzate overlooking Lake Varese with a magnificent view of the Monte Rosa Massif and the foothills of the Lombardy Alps, forty-five kilometers from Milan, forty kilometers from Lugano, Switzerland, and just twenty-five kilometers from Milan's Malpensa international airport. The entire area is filled with enchanting scenery, 17th-century chapels, a wealth of artistic gems, and many renowned golf courses. Originally the Locanda was a small 15th-century medieval settlement, complete with a piazza, post office, chemist's shop, and a grain storehouse. Later on, the village was transformed into a single country estate by the chemist, from whom the current owners, the Pomati family, are fifth-generation descendants. Carlotta Pomati and her son Paolo have converted the estate into a delightfully comfortable inn. The original tower, courtyard with well, and veranda have kept their unique charm. The dining room is remarkable for its 15th-century frescos, uncovered during renovation, and a 16th-century fireplace. The outer wall surrounding the Locanda has a visible niche in which an old fresco portraying the Madonna was placed toward the end of the 19th-century; today a statue stands in memory of the fresco which has since been erased by the passage of time. All the guestrooms are endowed with a traditional country feel but also feature the most modern comforts, which impart an elegant flavor and originality. Paolo, the owner-chef, meticulously prepares creative culinary works of art, featuring delicious regional and international dishes. Particular care is taken to select seasonal produce and the finest accompanying wines.

FINE POINTS

Our Family Loved Most: Close proximity to Malpensa airport, enabling our last night in Italy to be a memorable one instead of one spent in a typical airport establishment.
Rooms: 11 double rooms; 1 suite in the tower.
Food: Fresco dining room, seats 40; Weapon dining room, seats 12 & exclusive private dining room, only for 2.
Suggested Ages for Kids: All welcomed into our intimate atmosphere
Special Features: Meeting rooms; tower suite contains a sauna; garden; parking.

PALAZZO BARBARIGO SUL CANAL GRANDE

San Polo 2765 | Venice, Italy
Tel. +39 041740172 | Fax: +39 041740920
E-mail: palazzobarbarigo@mobygest.it | Web site: www.hotelphilosophy.net

Exclusive Luxury Family Offer: Complimentary fruit basket and *Dolcetti* (local biscuits typical of area) in room upon arrival. Please reference at time of reservation: LFHR-09.

PALAZZO BARBARIGO SUL CANAL GRANDE thrills visitors from the very first moments of approach. After a fifteen-minute water taxi ride from Piazzale Roma, you reach the palazzo's private dock, where you are greeted by a bellman who escorts you through a large sliding glass door into the reception area. The building occupies a prominent corner that extends into the Canal Grande, and other than its palatial yellow façade and a few placements of Murano glass, there is nothing traditional about this property. Quite the contrary. What makes Barbarigo so spectacular is an element of creativity that will delight those with a taste for the best in contemporary design. From the black marble floors of the reception area to the unique patterned gold wall of the main lounge, fine materials envelope the palazzo's entire interior. The rooms, which incorporate a masterful use of directed lighting, invoke awe. The floors, like the deck of a fine yacht, are strips of a soft gray wood; a contemporary bed is covered with two enormous white down comforters; a large flat-panel plasma television is held in an enormous black frame on the opposite wall; and a mirror in the bathroom features an embedded television. The service at Barbarigo surprises in the same way as the property's design. Used hand towels rarely remain for long, and the Bang & Olufsen telephones in each room can be used to summon the concierge at any hour. Within minutes by foot to the Rialto Bridge and Piazza San Marco, the property's location is prime, and strolling the neighborhood provides some of the city's top shopping. The Art Deco–style bar provides breakfast as well as light meals and snacks, and the front desk will be happy to recommend the best restaurants in the vicinity.

FINE POINTS

Our Family Loved Most: The hotel's sophisticated atmosphere and attentive staff made us feel like VIPs, and its central location right on the canal put us only minutes from the thick of things in Venice.
Rooms: 18 rooms, 6 deluxe junior suites.
Food: Bar and lounge serving cocktails as well as a breakfast buffet and light meals and snacks; in-room breakfast service.
Suggested Age for Kids: All ages welcome, but maximum occupancy per room is 2 adults and 1 child up to 11 years of age.
Special Features: 24-hour front desk; Internet service; room service; babysitting/childcare services; fitness room; water taxi service.

ROYAL HOTEL SANREMO

80, Corso Imperatrice | 18038 - Sanremo - Liguria, Italy

Tel. +39 01845391 | Fax: +39 0184661445

E-mail: royal@royalhotelsanremo.com | Web site: www.royalhotelsanremo.com

Exclusive Luxury Family Offer: THE ROYAL FAMILY WELCOME: Fruit basket and a bottle of Italian sparkling wine in room upon arrival. Please reference at time of reservation: LFHR-09.

ROYAL HOTEL SANREMO is located on the Italian Riviera of Flowers just south of the chic resort towns of Monte-Carlo, Nice, Cannes, and the French Riviera, only minutes from the center of Sanremo with its exclusive boutiques of the finest Italian fashion and its famous Sanremo Casino. Every guest is cordially welcomed upon arrival, most by name, for they return time and again. Truly an elite, time-honored resort, the hotel is surrounded by a luxuriant subtropical park of sixteen thousand square meters with a heated (27°C/82°F) seawater swimming pool offering impressive cascading views over the Mediterranean. The guest rooms are brilliantly decorated with only the finest amenities, many with breathtaking views; the penthouse level, especially, offers stunning views over the sea. Sun beds, umbrellas, and cabins are available to guests at a lido opposite the hotel, free of charge, according to availability.

The new state-of-the-art Royal Wellness features high-end treatments like Carita and Decléor, massage, a wet zone, plus fitness room and hair stylist. The Bar delle Rose is elegantly positioned beneath a magnificent frescoed ceiling providing a cozy place to relax with an afternoon tea, espresso, light fare, or a before-dinner aperitif. Whether poolside at Corallina, on the veranda of Fiori di Murano or at a candlelit table with a view of the sea and sunset at Il Giardino, dining here is an enchanting experience, distinguished by five-star services refined by a passion to generate the unsurpassed Mediterranean and international cuisine in the table d'hôte and à la carte menus. After dinner, cigar aficionados are certain to appreciate the elegant smoking lounge. Once the home of European royalty and aristocracy, the Royal Hotel Sanremo still remains the perfect place to stay between Monte-Carlo and Portofino.

FINE POINTS

Our Family Loved Most: Genuine warmth, caring service, with flawless cuisine amid one of the most luxurious resorts on the Italian Riviera of Flowers.
Rooms: 126 rooms and suites.
Food: Corallina pool bar; Bar delle Rose; Fiori di Murano; and Il Giardino.
Suggested Ages for Kids: All ages.
Special Features: Royal Wellness with high-end treatments like Carita and Decléor, massage, wet zone, plus fitness room and hair stylist; elegant smoking lounge; children's playroom and playgrounds; "Smile Club" for children with attendant in high season; babysitting on request; convention and banqueting facilities; tennis court; mini-golf; Wi-Fi Internet; private parking and garage; fuel station; transfers; car rental; 24-hour service; laundry and dry cleaning; water sports nearby; 18-hole golf course 5 km from hotel offering a 20 percent reduction on greens fees.

SAN CLEMENTE PALACE HOTEL & RESORT

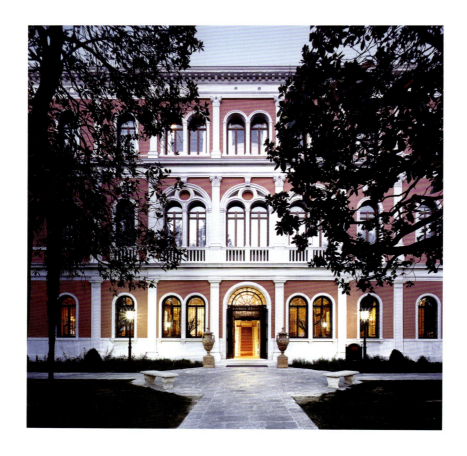

Isola di San Clemente 1 | San Marco, 30124 | Venice, Italy
Tel. +39 0412445001 | Fax: +39 0412445800
E-mail: sanclemente@thi.it | Web site: www.sanclemente.thi.it

Exclusive Luxury Family Offer: Classic suite available at special pricing for a family of 4 (two adults and two children up to age 14) with a minimum 2 nights' stay in low and shoulder season and 3 nights' stay in high season. Price: from €900 (high season); from €500 (shoulder season); and from €400 (low season). Please reference at time of reservation: LFHR-09.

SAN CLEMENTE PALACE HOTEL & RESORT occupies the entirety of San Clemente Island, an oasis of peace and tranquility situated in the Venetian lagoon only a few minutes by motorboat from St. Mark's Square. Formerly a patrician residence, pilgrim's rest, and monastery, the island has been transformed into an exclusive full-service luxury resort. Ample gardens and open space ensure an aura of privacy for couples seeking a romantic adventure, while generous accommodations—two hundred rooms and suites—make this the perfect spot for traveling families and groups meeting for conventions or special occasions. The carefully preserved Church of San Clemente, built in 1131, makes an ideal wedding destination, and the Palace itself features scenic courtyards, custom menus, and impeccable professional service. Whatever your reason for visiting, be sure to indulge in a bit of pampering at the La Perla della Laguna beauty and wellness club, which uses products based on freeze-dried algae and seawater. Take a water taxi back to the mainland to tour Venice, or while on the island enjoy the spectacular views of St. Mark's; just about every spot, including the rooms, overlooks something breathtaking. There are three restaurants at the Palace. Breakfast is served in the elegant 18th-century Gli Arazzi halls, while the Le Maschere restaurant is more informal. La Laguna near the swimming pool offers buffet service, and the elegant Ca' dei Frati has a refined *a la carte* menu. Le Conchiglie is an outdoor bar in San Clemente's century-old park next to the sports area, swimming pool, and tennis courts. Gli Specchi American bar is the place for cocktails, coffees, refined teas, pastries, and a quick snack or salad. Each restaurant has its own wine list that features the best in international, national, and regional vintages.

FINE POINTS

Our Family Loved Most: Having the best of both worlds: one minute enjoying the serenity and privacy of the island, the next being able to arrive in the heart of Venice thanks to a quick shuttle ride to Piazza San Marco.
Rooms: 200 rooms and suites with ultramodern amenities.
Food: 24-hour room service; 2 bars serving drinks, snacks, ice cream, and salads; 3 restaurants from casual to formal.
Suggested Age for Kids: All ages.
Special Features: La Boutique, selling exclusive Italian-made clothing, accessories, and beauty products; La Perla della Laguna beauty and wellness club; courtesy line of Laura Tonatto fragrances, designed exclusively for San Clemente Palace; Internet connection; meeting rooms with state-of-the-art technical equipment can host up to 350 people; wedding and special events planning; outdoor swimming pool; tennis courts; pitch and putt golf course; 24-hour shuttle service by boat to and from Piazza San Marco.

VILLA LUPPIS

Via San Martino, 34 | 33080 Rivarotta di Pasiano (Pordenone) | Italy
Tel. +39 0434626969 | Fax +39 0434626228
E-mail: hotel@villaluppis.it | Web site: www.villaluppis.it

Exclusive Luxury Family Offer: VENETIAN WINE TASTING: With a minimum stay of 3 nights, includes visit to a winery located in a beautiful Venetian villa only 10 minutes from Villa Luppis, with wine tasting. Valid all year. Please reference at time of reservation: LFHR-09.

VILLA LUPPIS was once known as San Martino Ripea Ruptae, the name of the monastery that was built here by the Camaldolite monks at the beginning of the 11th century. It is situated on the convergence of the rivers Livenza and Meduna and just forty minutes north of Venice. The estate was restored in 1500 after the destructive war between the Republic of Venice and the house of Hapsburgs, then purchased by the Chiozza/Luppis family at the beginning of 1800. It was transformed into a superb country house among an elegant estate where the family carried out their industrial and diplomatic activities. Today, the estate recalls the splendor and atmosphere of former times, as it is still run by the Luppis family. Stefania and Giorgio Ricci Luppis thoroughly refurbished the property, opening its doors as a hotel in 1993. The essence of the original home has been maintained by using the family's period antiques and valuable paintings as the backdrop to this fascinating villa rich in history. The guestrooms are all distinctively designed to elicit a warm home-like feeling, but the suites are more spacious, with individual characteristic features; the Antique Suite boasts century-old beamed ceiling, the Blue Junior Suite has a little lounge with a window opening onto the rose gardens, while the Pink Suite contains Louis XVI-style period furniture with a French fresco plus a balcony overlooking the park. Enjoy your day discovering exceptional Friuli wine cellars, ham and cheese factories, and the many splendid castles. Or simply relax at the swimming pool. The exquisitely prepared food is a superb integration of tradition with an abundant selection of international recipes.

FINE POINTS

Our Family Loved Most: The exceptional charm in a formal atmosphere with attentive, first-class hotel staff available to arrange anything you may desire.
Rooms: 39 rooms; 6 suites.
Food: Gourmet restaurant serving creative dishes.
Suggested Ages for Kids: All ages welcome, although the hotel seeks to offer a very quiet atmosphere for all guests to enjoy.
Special Features: Swimming pool; tennis; gym; bicycles; piano bar; daily shuttle service to/from Venice Piazzale Roma; shuttle service between Marco Polo airport in Venice on request; 3- to 5-day cooking classes; wine tasting suggested as a complete lunch or dinner, with the pairing of different wines; organized cultural and historic itineraries of the territory; discount shopping card; greens fees; ski pass; meeting rooms; renowned Mosaic School of Spilmbergo, skiing, golf, horseback riding, and skating all nearby.

The cities shown in red represent locations of Luxury Family Hotels & Resorts.

Central Italy

Central Italy is the country's geographic and cultural heart, embodying all the qualities we would consider quintessentially Italian. Certainly, a tour of this region is a must on any Italian travel itinerary, whether that includes Tuscany's sun-drenched vineyards, olive groves, and charming villages, Marche's lively coastal towns, Umbria's historic Etruscan sites, or the magnificent art cities of Florence, Rome, Pisa, and Siena. Hidden treasures off the beaten path abound as well, rewarding the intrepid traveler with an ever-expanding appreciation for this abundant land. Your culinary adventures will be enlightening. Tuscany is of course famous as a gourmand's paradise, as is Emilia-Romagna and Umbria, home to some of the world's great cheeses and pastas. Marche and Abruzzo offer outstanding seafood, and Lazio provides distinctively unique local wines.

Emilia-Romagna

Known for its cuisine, diversity of landscapes, and a wealth of historic towns, this region attracts visitors seeking a variety of amusements. The coastal towns of Rimini and Misano Adriatico are a summer paradise with miles of sandy beaches. Just about any outdoor activity is readily available from these locations, including deep-sea fishing, hot springs, mud baths, and water sports. Additionally, these towns boast a wealth of restaurants and nightclubs. The charming city of Ravenna, capital of the Western Roman Empire in the 5th and 6th centuries, is situated on the Adriatic coast halfway between Venice and Florence, and is best known for the brilliant mosaic ornamentation of its Byzantine churches and tombs. On the banks of the river Po is the superb Renaissance city of Ferrara with its *palazzos* (palaces), shops, cafés, and narrow medieval streets. In San Marino, cars are forbidden, which facilitates the exploration of this marvelous medieval city by foot. There is much to discover when wandering along winding narrow streets lined with red-roofed stone houses, medieval walls, and fortresses. Bologna is not only the capital and heart of Emilia-Romagna, it is also home to such notable artists such as Carracci, Parmigianini, and the memorable

A typical delicatessen in Emilia-Romagna, filled with an assortment of salami, ham, cheese, fruit, vegetables, wine, and olive oils. It sits adjacent to restaurant Antica Locanda del Falco in the Piacenza area.

Pavarotti. Lamborghini and Ferrari sports cars and Ducati motorcycles are manufactured here. Cobbled streets provide pathways to the city's Romanesque and Gothic architecture, as well as medieval *palazzos* and majestic towers.

Classic Cuisine: Emilia-Romagna is politically considered a single region, but is in fact two, especially with respect to cuisine. Emilia, the region's capital, is north of Bologna. Romagna is located to the south. As such, Bologna embodies distinct characteristics of both Emilia and Romagna. The foods of both areas are hearty and feature the three main cooking fats of butter, oil, and lard. *Bologna la grassa* (Bologna the Fat) is a title the city has acquired for its characteristically rich cuisine, the quality of its pork products, and the richness of its pastas. *Tagliatelle* and *lasagna* are favorites, but *tortellini* is one of its most renowned dishes, served stuffed with Parmesan cheese, pork, raw ham, turkey breast, egg, and *mortadella* (minced pork meat). Emilia, specifically Parma, is the home of salamis. It is thought that Parma's *prosciutto* (cured ham) is sweeter than that of any other region in Italy. *Culatello di Zibello* (cured leg of an adult hog) is another specialty. Modena features the *Zampone* and *Cotechino di Modena,* which are cured meat products made from a combination of pork taken from striated muscle fibers, pork fat, pigskin, and different seasonings. Romagna's food preparation on the other hand embraces aromatic herbs and the use of skewers to roast seafood, chicken, game, other meats, and a variety of sausages. Vegetables are simply but flavorfully prepared in dishes such as *asparagi aila parmigianna* (baked asparagus) or *melanzane marinate* (marinated eggplants). Emilia-Romagna has two other great culinary contributions: balsamic vinegar, which has been made in Modena for centuries, and *Parmigiano Reggiano*, the unsurpassed king of cheese, made in the provinces of Parma, Reggio, and Emilia for over seven hundred years.

Divine Wine: The lush, fertile plains of the Po valley are among the most intensively farmed land in Italy. Most support orchards, but the land around Modena, Reggio dell'Emilia, and Bologna is carpeted with Lambrusco vines. The vast if diminishing Lambrusco production—dominated by several enormous cooperatives—is

OPPOSITE: A dining experience in Florence at Hotel Regency's Relais Le Jardin is sure to be an utter pleasure. THIS PAGE: Within the ancient wine cellar of Emilia-Romagna's Antica Locanda del Falco restaurant are located thousands of bottles from the most important Italian production zones, along with a fair selection of foreign wines.

not all destined for large, screw-top bottles of red wine: there are any number of bottles that contain the genuine article. Whether from the DOC zones of Grasparossa di Castelvetro, Salamino di Santa Croce, Reggiano, or Sorbara, real Lambrusco is a frothing, purple drink with high acidity and a touch of sweetness that perfectly complements the rich cooking of Emilia. The rest of Emilia-Romagna's wine tends to come from the Apennine foothills that cut across the southern part of the region. To the west, the Piacenza hills form the basis for the Colli Piacentini DOC, while those around Parma and Bologna are known as the Colli di Parma and Colli Bolognesi, respectively. In each of these zones, several different varietals or blends are designated separately under the DOC umbrella. In general, the quality from grapes such as Trebbiano, Barbera, Malvasia, and even Chardonnay, Sauvignon, and Cabernet, is sound rather than exciting. To the east of Bologna, the Romagnan hills form the center for the Sangiovese, Trebbiano, and Albana di Romagna zones. The Albana grape produces a decent dry and an excellent sweet white wine, while the former two, once notable only for their lack of distinction, are today producing wines of increasing quality, especially Sangiovese.

Tuscany

Tuscany, *Toscana* in Italian, is the most well-known Italian region, and is distinguished by many small, picturesque hilltop towns. Most are situated on gently rolling hillsides amid vineyards and olive groves, winding roads, ancient villas, and castles. Florence, Pisa, Lucca, and Siena are the region's most well-known cities, and together they offer visitors many fascinating attractions. Florence is of course the renowned home of history's greatest artistic geniuses: Leonardo da Vinci, Michelangelo Buonarroti, and Filippo Brunelleschi. Their work, as well as that of many other generations of artists up to the present time, is featured in the scores of museums and public places scattered throughout the city. The Uffizi, the most select picture gallery in the world, displays Renaissance art featuring the works of da Vinci, Botticelli, Michelangelo, Raphael, Canaletto, and many more. Visit the

OPPOSITE: The roses, lavender, and mulberry trees perfectly complement the olive grove, vineyard, and woods at Castello di Vicarello, Tuscany. THIS PAGE: At Sapori del Lord Byron in Rome, the extremely talented chef demonstrates remarkable insight and respect for Italian cuisine while capturing its authentic vibrancy.

Rooms of the Planets at the Galleria Palatina. The Galleria dell'Accademia hosts very important collections of paintings along with well-known works by Michelangelo, including *Il Gigante*, more commonly known as the *Statue of David*. The collection at Stibbert's museum focuses on the history and traditions of various cultures, and includes weapons, armor, costumes, furnishings, and examples of the applied arts in the form of 16th- to 19th-century tapestries and paintings. Visit the Medici Chapel and the Buonarroti House, both of which contain sculptures by Michelangelo. The Museo degli Argenti, or Silver Museum, is located in Palazzo Pitti and houses various precious objects such as gems, cameos, semi-precious stones, ivories, jewels, and silver. In Pisa, the Leaning Tower is of course the main attraction. Lucca, the birthplace of Giacomo Puccini, is a charming walled city, and Siena, with its Piazza del Campo, is home to the world-famous Palio horse race. Venturing outside these municipalities will put you in the heart of some of the most authentic medieval villages and seaside towns: southeast of Florence, one finds Arezzo, Cortona, Montepulciano, and Montalcino; south of Florence and Siena is San Gimignano, Pienza, Pitigliano, Saturnia, Grosseto, and the island of Elba; northwest of Florence are located Lucca, Pisa, Forte dei Marmi, Pietrasanta, Viareggio, and Carrara.

Classic Cuisine: When you think of Italian cuisine, the highly publicized Tuscany most certainly comes to mind. Its approach to food has always been one of simplicity, founded on a love of wine, olive oil, and bread. Leftover bread is never wasted but used as the main ingredient for several common dishes. Most well known are *Panzanella* salad made with bread, tomato, onion, and olive oil, and *Ribollita*, a thick soup prepared with green vegetables, cabbage, beans, bread, and olive oil. Fresh pasta, particularly *parppardella, ravioli, pici,* and *tordelli* made with chestnuts, Pecorino cheese (usually sheep or goat), beans, prosciutto, basil, rosemary, marjoram, bay leaves, sage, parsley, and thyme, has been part of the Etruscan kitchen for centuries. Vegetables combined with fish, beans, and meats grilled over an open fire are regular fare on the Tuscan table. One such dish is *bistecca alla Fiorentina*, a thickly cut steak seasoned only with olive oil, salt, and pepper. Many Tuscan dishes center around vegetables such as artichokes, asparagus, fennel, peas, spinach, and mushrooms. Besides steak, Tuscan meat dishes include wild game and boar, duck, rabbit, and beef tripe. Although you will find dishes like *sogliola alla Florentine* (sole) on inland

THIS PAGE: The restaurant of Relais La Corte dei Papi serves a harmonic fusion of traditional Tuscan cuisine with an up-to-the-minute approach. OPPOSITE: Montepulciano is one of Tuscany's most beautiful medieval towns. It is still encircled by impressive, intact fortifications from the Renaissance era. Image courtesy Borgo Tre Rose.

menus, coastal Tuscan cuisine incorporates a wider variety of fish, as demonstrated in recipes such as *sarde in marinara* (marinated sardines), *Triglie alla livornese* (red mullet), and *cacciucco all livornese* (fish stew made in the Tuscan port of Livorno). Tuscany is known for several different desserts, but none are more famous than the simply delicious *biscotti* (hard cookie), made exclusively for dipping in sweet *Vin Santo* or espresso.

Divine Wine: The soul of Tuscany is the Sangiovese grape. Although its clones vary, the underlying style is always unique and distinct. With aromas of fresh tea and prunes, or plums or cherries, it is notably spicy, with nutmeg, clove, and cinnamon the most common characteristics. Many producers balance the major challenges of making a superior Sangiovese by including a proportion of the more consumer-friendly Cabernet Sauvignon grape, which is also grown in the region. The most famous red from the area is Chianti. No longer just ubiquitous Italian table wine in a strawcovered bottle, Chianti now boasts many high-quality, well-accepted producers, including Castello di Ama, Antinori, and Fontodi. No discussion of wine in the region is complete without mentioning the "super-Tuscans." Many quality Italian wines are not made in accordance with DOC or DOCG guidelines, and so take on the presumed lesser status of IGT. Most are either 100 percent Sangiovese or Sangiovese/Cabernet blends. They include such heralded and high-priced producers as Sassicaia and Tignanello. The primary white varieties in the region are Trebbiano Toscano and Malvasia, although most producers prefer to work with Chardonnay, albeit with very different results from French or New World Chardonnays. The unique wine of the region is *Vin Santo* or Holy Wine, traditionally offered when stepping from the hot summer sun into a cool Tuscan farmhouse, and it may also be considered a dessert wine. Typically, it is made with either Trebbiano or Malvasia grapes, but may contain both, and as much as 30 percent of other grapes, including Sangiovese. The grapes are left on mats to dry and shrivel before crushing. After fermentation, the wine is aged in small, sealed barrels for as little as three and as many as ten years.

Marche

This region lies on the eastern side of central Italy, between the Adriatic Sea and the Apennine Mountains. Many travelers who come to the Marche are looking for the "authentic" Italy, untarnished by crowds, but welcoming of outsiders. The hilltops are strewn with scenic towns and castles, some lending magnificent views all the way to the sea. The Marche is

typically known for its seaside beach resorts, the larger of which are now quite bustling and known for their lively, upbeat nightlife. Some main locations include Gabicce Mare, Pesaro, Fano, San Benedetto del Tronto, and Senigallia, famous for its "Velvet Beach." Monte Conero, however, with its white limestone cliffs and rocky coves, is unlike anything else along this section of Adriatic coastline. Here, the main towns are Urbino, an important city for visitors interested in fine Italian art and architecture; Ancona, with its busy seaport and main ferry connection to Croatia, Greece, and Turkey; Pesaro, an appealing seaside resort and a productive town with good shops and beaches; and Macerata, famous for its annual outdoor opera festival. Ascoli Piceno is southern Marche's epicenter, and its Renaissance-style main square, *Piazza del Popolo* ("Square of the People"), is considered one of the most beautiful in Italy. Long-established records indicate Ascoli Piceno was home to more than two hundred towers in the Middle Ages. Today, about fifty still exist.

Classic Cuisine: Pasta dishes reign supreme, particularly *tagliatelle* with a vegetable, fish, or meat *sugo* (sauce); *vincisgrassi*, rich baked lasagna with ground pork, mushrooms, and tomato and béchamel sauce, topped with truffles; and *passatelli*, strands of pasta made from breadcrumbs, Parmesan cheese, and egg cooked in broth. Mountain-cured ham and *grigliata mista di carne* (charcoal-grilled meat) are highly popular as well. Favorite meats include veal, rabbit, quail, pigeon, chicken, and goose, which are often cooked in a porchetta style like *coniglio in porchetta* (stuffed rabbit with fennel, garlic, and rosemary). Along the coast, fresh seafood is traditionally served, especially *brodetto,* a fish stew made with thirteen different varieties of fish. *Funghi* (mushroom), nuts, herbs, game, *tartufi bianco* (white truffles), and *tartufo nero pregiato* (black truffles) are widely used in the Marche. Pecorino di San Leo, a sheep's milk cheese, is exceptional, as is Casciotta d'Urbino, a crumbly, semi-cooked cheese made from a blend of whole sheep's milk and whole cow's milk.

Divine Wine: Sangiovese and Trebbiano are still the prevalent grapes of this region, but you can find some excellent Verdicchio whites and Montepulciano reds. The best Verdicchio wines come from producers that include Bucci, Garofoli, and Umani Ronchi. They are rich and viscous, making a good match for the local

THIS PAGE: Spello is one of the most charming medieval towns in Umbria and also one of the least crowded with tourists. OPPOSITE: La Bucaccia Ristorante creates a dining experience that is the perfect expression of Tuscan culinary traditions from the Arezzo area: simple, refined, and harmonious in proportion and taste.

fish-based dishes, especially when drunk young. Good Montepulciano wines come from Rosso Conero and Rosso Piceno Superiore. The area also produces some interesting and off-beat wines, including a sparkling red made in a sweet and dry style, called Vernaccia di Serrapetrona.

Umbria

Located in the middle of Italy, Umbria is the only region in the central part of the country without a coastline. Umbria is often referred to as the "green heart of Italy," with its medieval towns and characteristic lush, green rolling hills. The prominent towns include Orvieto, with its magnificent Gothic *duomo* (cathedral) and glittering façade; Spoleto, home of the *Festival dei Due Mondi* (Festival of Two Worlds), a worldwide attraction that includes music, dance, and theatre scenes; and Assisi, the birthplace of St. Francis. Perugia is the region's capital and a very important Etruscan city, whose stunning architecture includes the Etruscan Arch and the Etruscan Well. Top museums include Perugia's National Gallery, with the largest collection of Umbrian art in the world and a comprehensive collection of Perugian paintings. Imaginative palaces, monasteries, and churches enhance the region's distinctive hillside towns of Gubbio, Spoleto, Todi, Spello, Città di Castello, and more. Many of these architectural gems are also known for fine handmade ceramics and savory black truffles. Umbria is home to Lake Trasimeno, where you can take a jaunt by boat to one of its many islands with their beautiful beaches.

Classic Cuisine: Umbria's food consists of some basic ingredients: premium olive oil, Durum wheat pasta, hog, lamb, and *colombaccio* (pigeon). Two specialties of the region are *mazzafegati*, sausages made from hog's liver, pine nuts, orange peel, raisins, and sugar, as well as *tartufo nero* (black truffles), grown beneath the earth and served over everything including Pecorino cheese. Due to their limited quantities, these truffles are one of the most expensive foods in the world. Many variations of homemade egg pasta, notably *tagliatelle, ciriole,* and *stringozzi,* are prepared in a decadent black truffle sauce unique to the region. Umbria is also responsible for the production of much of the dried pasta consumed throughout Italy. Umbrians cook a wide range of foods that incorporate fish, meat, game, vegetables, and rice, as well as a variety of herbs and spices. A classic menu may include *frittata ai funghi* (mushroom omelet), *minestra di riso* (rice soup with lentils), and *pollo alla cacciatore* (chicken with capers and olives).

Divine Wine: Grecheto is the only native white grape varietal of note in this region. It makes a punchy, nutty wine and is most often blended with Trebbiano. Orvieto is the most important wine of southern Umbria, and is normally blended with Trebbiano as well. Sagrantino is one of Italy's greatest red grape varietals, but it is normally only found around the town of Montefalco. It produces deep-colored, tannic, and strong wines that are intense and long finishing. Outside the DOCG, it is blended with Sangiovese, but the powerhouse wines from Antonelli and Caprai are notable examples of this unique grape.

Lazio

The cradle of Roman civilization, Lazio is home to its greatest manifestation, the Eternal City. Most certainly, Rome is not to be missed during one's travels to central Italy. Principal sights of interest include Vatican City and its museums that house Raphael's rooms; the Sistine Chapel; the Basilica of St. Peter and St. Peter's square; Villa Borghese; the Colosseum; the Roman Forum; Piazza Navona; Piazza Farnese; the Pantheon; the Jewish Ghetto; Trastevere; and the outdoor market at Campo de' Fiori.

Also, put aside some time for exploring the exclusive shops along the Via Veneto and around the Spanish Steps. According to tradition, throwing a coin into the Trevi Fountain ensures you will return to the Eternal City. Around Rome, also visit: Tivoli, best known for Villa d'Este with its unique gardens, gravitational water system, and fountains; Frascati and Grottaferrata, located in the Castelli Romani hills overlooking the city of Rome, which have been a favorite summer retreat of the Romans since antiquity; Ostia Antica, the old Roman port with some of the oldest remains in Lazio; Lake Bracciano, the eighth-largest lake in Italy, with its medieval village of Trevignano, many lakeside cafes, and restaurants; and the Orsini Odescalchi castle dating from the 12th century. Water sports are popular in this area as well. Noteworthy Etruscan cities worth visiting are Cerveteri, Tarquinia, and Viterbo. Visit the Tyrrenian Sea at Civitavecchia, especially in summer, when you can relax on sandy beaches and snorkel the reefs that are common along its coastline.

Classic Cuisine: The traditional food of Rome and Lazio has always made abundant use of fresh, seasonal produce grown

OPPOSITE: Hotel Eden's rooftop restaurant, La Terrazza dell'Eden, offers a magnificent panoramic view of Rome and serves delectable Mediterranean cuisine with a wine list fit for a connoisseur. THIS PAGE: A gastronomical journey awaits all guests who dine at our featured hotels and resorts. Image courtesy Hotel Regency's Relais Le Jardin Restaurant.

throughout the countryside: artichokes in spring, mushrooms in autumn, and luscious figs and watermelon in the summer months. Many Roman dishes are well seasoned with onions, garlic, rosemary, sage, and bay leaves. Pasta takes on its own character in Roman specialties, like *Bucatini all'amatriciana* with tomatoes and a spicy bacon sauce, *Fettuccine alla Romana, linguini* with a chicken liver sauce, and *penne all'arrabbiata* with a spicy chili pepper sauce. Meat dishes include *saltimbocca alla romana* (veal cutlets with sage) and *abbacchio alla Romana* (braised lamb with a garlic sauce). *Carciofi* (artichokes) are well regarded and may be prepared in one of two ways: *alla giudia* (Jewish style) or *alla Romana* (Roman style), cooked in oil with garlic and parsley. Possibly the most familiar Roman specialty is *Bruschetta*, toasted bread rubbed with a clove of garlic then drizzled with olive oil and salt, or chopped fresh tomatoes. Pecorino, a flavorful sheep's milk cheese, is often incorporated into dishes, while a mild Ricotta is used as a filling for pizzas and as an ingredient in the Roman dessert *torta di ricotta*.

Divine Wine: Most of the wines produced in Lazio are also consumed in Lazio, with little being exported to other regions or outside of Italy. The primary grapes are Trebbiano and Malvasia. Producers in Frascati and Montefiascone are using other grapes, including Chardonnay and Viognier, to generate wines of more interest. Frascati is still considered a commodity wine, but an increasing proportion is now of better quality. Noted producers include Galesco, Colli di Catone, Castel de Paolis, Fontana Candida, and Villa Simone. The unique wine of this zone is Est! Est! Est! di Montefiascone, produced mainly from Trebbiano Toscano, Malvasia Toscana, and Trebbiano Giallo. The story goes that during the 12th century, a traveling bishop sent an aide ahead of his route to find the best drink along the way. The aide was so impressed by a wine he found at a local inn near Montefiascone that he chalked "Here it is!" three times on the door of the establishment so his master would not miss it. Given the opportunity, neither should you.

Abruzzo

This region, together with Molise, forms the "ankle" of Italy. It hugs the southeastern seaboard with expansive sandy beaches extending from the north along the Adriatic, directly southward to Pescara. Traveling west from the sea, this region becomes dominated by the Apennines Mountains. Abruzzo is usually thought of as being out-of-the-way and isolated, marked only by desolate hill towns clinging to the sides of mountains. Abruzzo, along with some of the other

OPPOSITE: Borgo Tre Rose is located in the heart of Tenuta Tre Rose, a prestigious wine company that produces high-quality Tuscan wines. THIS PAGE: Lucignanello Bandini's products are of outstanding quality and made by time-honored methods; Pecorino cheeses from the Pienza pastures are now in high demand among the world's most discerning gourmands.

southern regions, epitomizes a way of life impervious to change for centuries. Here, you will find a land of shepherds, uncultivated countryside, and desolate castles. Sulmona, an active town with about twenty-five thousand residents, sits four hundred meters above sea level in the center of Abruzzo. It has narrow streets, tree-lined *piazzas* (squares) with imposing houses, especially along Via dell'Ospedale, and displays fine architecture festooned with carved windows and remnants of frescos and sculptures. You will find shops selling blankets, shawls, and sweaters, all made with local wool by the women of Sulmona, whose handiwork is legendary. To the east of Sulmona are the sixty-one peaks and heavily wooded valleys of Maiella National Park, offering climbing, skiing, walking, and bird watching. Abruzzo National Park, with its fertile landscape, towering peaks, rivers, lakes, and woodlands, is one of the most important in all of Europe. It provides refuge for more than forty species of mammals, thirty kinds of reptiles, and three hundred species of birds, including the white-backed woodpecker and golden eagle. Along with opportunities for paddling, horseback riding, and skiing, a widespread array of trails provides hikers of all levels of experience with miles of exploration.

Classic Cuisine: The food in Abruzzo is memorable. Their cuisine is highly flavored, mainly with *pepperoncini* (hot red peppers), olive oil, wine, garlic, rosemary, and aromatic saffron, which is considered to be the most symbolic ingredient of Abruzzo's time-honored cuisine. Mushrooms are integrated into almost everything. Shepherding remains the daily way to make a living; therefore, lamb, kid, sheep, and mountain goat are the primary meats served roasted or grilled. Many people still raise their own pigs, which produce tasty, lean meat and flavorsome *salami*. In seaport areas, a variety of fresh fish is incorporated into savory soups. Pasta is most often the first course and *maccheroni alla chitarra* (guitar pasta) is the most typical, wherein sheets of egg dough are cut with a flat rolling pin on a wooden box with strings. Pecorino d'Abruzzo, the local sheep's cheese, and Burrata, spheres of a luscious Mozzarella-like cheese with a soft buttery center, are specialties of this region. *Scrippelle*, or crêpes, are traditionally served as dessert, but in Abruzzo, they are rolled with tasty fillings, placed into broths, or served with cheese, vegetables, and meat.

Divine Wine: One-quarter of Abruzzo's wine production centers in Biferno, whose output is either consumed locally or sent to other parts of Italy for blending into other wines. The exceptions include Barone Conacchia, Maciarelli, and Valentini, all of which produce noted wines of character and depth.

ALBERGO DEL SOLE AL PANTHEON

Piazza della Rotonda, 63 – 00186 | Rome, Italy

Tel. +39 066780441 | Fax: +39 0669940689

E-mail: info@hotelsolealpantheon.com | Web site: www.hotelsolealpantheon.com

Exclusive Luxury Family Offer: Fruit basket and a bottle of Italian sparkling wine in room upon arrival. Please reference at time of reservation: LFHR-09.

HOTEL ALBERGO DEL SOLE AL PANTHEON occupies a prime spot just in front of the Pantheon in the charming Piazza della Rotonda close to Navona Square, Trevi Fountain, and the Spanish Steps. Warmly welcoming travelers since 1467, it is officially the oldest hotel in Rome. Painstaking renovations have restored this historic jewel back to its original 15th-century glory, albeit with a myriad of modern, four-star hotel amenities. It's certainly thrilling to occupy the same space once enjoyed by Jean Paul Sartre, Frederich Nietzsche, and Simone de Beauvoir, and to contemplate the fact that this is where opera composer Mascagni stayed the night his work "La Cavalliera Rusticana" premiered. Adding to this allure are a host of amenities that make this a truly luxuriant haven from which to enjoy Rome. Each of the hotel's thirty-three rooms are distinctive in design and décor, boasting elegant touches like beautiful desks made from Peperino, a local dark green stone. The highly professional concierge staff happily provides maps, directions, museum times, restaurant advice, and can organize any excursion in or around the city. Not only is the hotel a few steps away from the Pantheon, it is also surrounded by narrow, ancient side streets full of fascinating shops, bars, restaurants, and cafes, all off the beaten tourist path and definitely worth exploring. One of the hotel's most charming features is its roof-garden breakfast room. The buffet breakfast—reportedly one of the best in Rome—features delicacies like fresh Ricotta cheese and homemade cakes and pastries. Exceptional nearby restaurants include Mancini, La Rosetta, and Agata e Romeo, among others. After dining out, return to the hotel to relax with a cocktail or a glass of one of the many regional wines.

FINE POINTS

Our Family Loved Most: Our guestroom with superior view overlooking the Pantheon.
Rooms: 33 rooms, including superior (overlooking the Pantheon), standard (interior), 4 junior suites, 7 family suites in the annex 50 meters from the hotel.
Food: Bar and lounge; lavish breakfast buffet; many excellent restaurants nearby.
Suggested Age for Kids: All ages; free up to 6 years when sharing room with parents.
Special Features: Buffet breakfast; private pick-up from the airport upon request; 24-hour reception and concierge; fax services; Internet available 24/7 in lobby; library and sitting room; Jacuzzi tubs in all rooms; laundry service; motorbikes and bicycles for hire; museum entrance/ticketing service at front desk; currency exchange; children's activities; pets welcome

ALBERGO PIETRASANTA

Via Garibaldi 35 | Marina Di Pietrasanta 55045, Italy
Tel. +39 0584793726 | Fax: +39 0584793728
E-mail: info@albergopietrasanta.com | Web site: www.albergopietrasanta.com

Exclusive Luxury Family Offer: Minimum stay two nights in a junior suite; one night free in their sister property in Florence, La Residenza del Moro. Valid upon availability all year round. Please reference at time of reservation: LFHR-09.

ALBERGO PIETRASANTA is situated in a magnificent seventeenth-century palace known as Palazzo Barsanti Bonetti, in the historical center of Tuscany's town of Pietrasanta, just a few steps from chic boutiques, restaurants, pizzerias, and cafés. This culturally rich artistic town is a delight to wander. Visit the medieval piazza, historic monuments, beautiful cathedrals, or tour fascinating workshops of the local artisans. What's more, the major art cities of Florence, Pisa, Lucca, Carrara, as well as the charming coastal towns of the Cinque Terre and Portofino, are near. The lovely beaches of Versilia can effortlessly be reached by bicycle or the hotel's shuttle service, both of which are complimentary. The quality staff of Pietrasanta, led by general manager Barbara Pardini, will embrace your family with genuine loving care and the meticulous service of a first-class hotel. Its exceptional collection of contemporary art displayed throughout offers an exclusive view of Italian paintings from the middle of the twentieth century to present day. Every facet of this historical palace was decorated and furnished individually to create its own unique allure, resulting in a modern masterpiece abounding with evidence of its important past. A lovely interior veranda faces landscaped gardens with century-old trees that connect the main building to the adjacent converted stables. This area is quite a romantic setting to enjoy an espresso, a cocktail from the casual bar, or breakfast, which is available until two in the afternoon. There is no restaurant per se, but the kitchen is always open to serve a fine selection of light cuisine either in the courtyard or the privacy of your room. Then again, outstanding ristorantes are plentiful—just steps from Albergo Pietrasanta's prime location.

FINE POINTS

Our Family Loved Most: A luxurious hotel from which to tour Tuscany's rich coastal towns and famous medieval hamlets.
Rooms: 19 rooms; 4 spacious suites, all with original frescoes or tromps d'oeil, fresh flowers, and complimentary Vin Santo and Cantucci.
Food: 24-hour light food service; restaurants abound in Pietrasanta, and the Enoteca Marcucci, with its excellent Tuscan food and wine, is located across the street. Reservations suggested.
Suggested Ages for Kids: All ages.
Special Features: Complimentary shuttle service to and from beach; free use of bikes; gym; beauty treatments; picnic baskets. Nearby: private Italian lessons; beaches of Versilia; paragliding; golf; marble sculpturing courses; cooking courses; Puccini Opera Festival (July/August); Breakfast on the Beach (May, June, October).

BORGO TRE ROSE

Via I Palazzi, 5 | 53040 Montepulciano - Valiano (Si), Italy
Tel. +39 057872491 | Fax: +39 0578724227
E-mail: info@borgotrerose.it | Web site: www.borgotrerose.it

Exclusive Luxury Family Offer: SECRETS OF THE CUERDA SECA ART: In the studio at Borgo Tre Rose, learn the techniques of the Cuerda Seca, or decoration of glazes on terra cotta and proper oven cooking techniques. The package includes: 2 half-day lessons; 1 visit to the terra cotta museum; all essential materials; your completed works of art to take home; 3 nights' accommodations inclusive of fruit basket and bottle of their red wine in room upon arrival, and international buffet breakfast. From €357 per person based upon availability. Please reference at time of reservation: LFHR-09.

BORGO TRE ROSE is located in the heart of the splendid Tuscan countryside in the hills between Montepulciano and Cortona. The complex is actually six restored homes in the center of a village established in medieval times that today constitutes the wine producing business of Tenute Tre Rose. Surrounded by green farmland, extensive vineyards, and ancient olive and cypress groves, this is the classic Tuscan farm holiday. With its down-to-earth guest rooms featuring exposed beams and terra cotta floors to the accommodating service, Borgo Tre Rose provides guests with the sense of living among a well-preserved history and way of life. One can't help but relax here, exploring the hilltop village or discovering Tuscan culinary and artisan traditions with onsite cooking lessons and instruction in traditional porcelain painting. Kids of all ages will find plenty to do under the Tuscan sun as well: taking a refreshing dip in the sparkling pool, playing a rousing game of tennis or ping pong, biking in the mountains, climbing the rock wall, or enjoying the easy company of the other families. Borgo Tre Rose is also nearby many regional villages and attractions, and is only fourteen kilometers from Montepulciano and sixteen kilometers from Cortona. Authentic Tuscan cuisine is available breakfast, lunch, and dinner at the well-situated on-site restaurant with panoramic terrace. And, you couldn't ask for a better spot from which to sample the best regional wines. Tenuta Tre Rose has earned its prestige producing the highest-quality Tuscan wines, including Vin Santo (the typical Tuscan dessert wine), Nobile di Montepulciano wines Simposio and La Villa, as well as its excellent whites, Renaio and Busillis.

FINE POINTS

Our Family Loved Most: Quintessential Tuscan views in an unpretentious atmosphere.
Rooms: 40 rooms, including studios for 2 with separate entrance; classics for 2–3 with separate entrance; and suites for 2–4 with balcony or terrace and separate entrance.
Suggested Ages for Kids: All ages.
Food: Bar/lounge; breakfast buffet; lunch and dinner at on-site restaurant.
Special Features: Two banquet halls; full conference, meeting, and event facilities with all state-of-the art audio/visual equipment; wedding and special events planning and catering; panoramic terrace that seats 80; swimming pool; tennis courts; ping pong; can organize rock climbing (on rock climbing wall), hot air balloon rides, mountain bike rentals, and excursions; cooking and porcelain painting courses; outdoor summer concerts; playground for children; nearby lake for sport fishing; guided tours of the winery with wine tasting.

CASTELLO DI GARGONZA

Località Gargonza | 52048 Monte San Savino, Italy
Tel. +39 0575847021 | Fax: +39 0575847054
E-mail: info@gargonza.it | Web site: www.gargonza.it | Member of: www.abitarelastoria.it

Exclusive Luxury Family Offer: 10 percent discount applicable to stays of three nights or more; fruit basket and a bottle of Italian sparkling wine in room upon arrival. Please reference at time of reservation: LFHR-09.

CASTELLO DI GARGONZA is a 13th-century fortified village nestled in the heart of Tuscany, only nine kilometers from Monte San Savino and twenty-eight kilometers from Arezzo. This one-time fortification was also the spot where, in 1303, Dante Alighieri spent a few days of his exile. In the 1600s, it was organized as a communal farm. In 1970, Roberto Guicciardini Corsi Salviati lovingly restored the property into a bed and breakfast with rooms and apartments in thirteen original buildings. Maintaining their authentic structure and atmosphere, each offers the utmost in modern services and amenities. Beautiful and tranquil, the village and its natural surroundings make for an ideal retreat. Enjoy quiet time in the lovely gardens, take in the fresh air and spectacular views from the pool, enjoy a snack inside the lemon tree greenhouse, or tour the village's ancient olive press and cellar. Staff will also gladly book excursions to nearby ancient Etruscan sites, wineries and *oleotecas*, or to view Renaissance master Piero della Francesca's many works located in spots throughout the nearby villages. A spacious rental villa, common areas, and meeting and banquet rooms can accommodate just about any size family or business get-together, and the Romanic church and beautifully cultivated gardens make for a storybook wedding locale. While several of the apartment-sized rooms are equipped with kitchenettes, dinner at the property's La Torre di Gargonza Restaurant, located in an ancient tractor shed, is not to be missed. Chef Andrea Russo focuses on authentic Tuscan dishes crafted from simple, regional ingredients at the peak of their seasonal freshness. Specialties like Tuscan vegetable soup, grilled wild boar in juniper sauce, and *torta della nonna* (granny's cake) are accompanied by a wine list of over sixty regional varieties.

FINE POINTS

Our Family Loved Most: The blend of history and tranquility that make this an ideal spot for a quiet retreat or a special gathering.
Rooms: 14 rooms; 8 apartments for 2–3 people; 6 apartments for 4–6 people; 1 apartment for up to 8 people; 1 villa for up to 10 people.
Food: Snack bar; bar; Olive Press Cellar breakfast buffet; La Torre di Gargonza restaurant.
Suggested Ages for Kids: All ages.
Special Features: Television lounge with satellite TV; breakfast room; gardens; swimming pool; Wi-Fi Internet; fee transfer to and from airport and train station; guided tour reservations; laundry service.

CASTELLO DI MAGONA

Via di Venturina, 27, 57021 | Campiglia Marittima | Livorno, Italy
Tel. +39 0565851235 | Fax: +39 0565855127
E-mail: relais@castellodimagona.it | Web site: www.castellodimagona.it | Member of: www.abitarelastoria.it

Exclusive Luxury Family Offer: 10 percent discount applicable to weekly rental rates. Please reference at time of reservation: LFHR-09.

CASTELLO DI MAGONA is a restored 16th-century castle that exudes historic ambience while also impressing guests with its meticulous attention to 21st-century luxury and service. Located on the Etruscan coast between Siena and Lucca, the castle was once the residence of Leopold II Grand Duke of Tuscany. It is currently owned by Cesare Mercial, a gracious and charming host whose personal motto is: "This is my house and you are my guests." Accommodations include ten rooms of which six are suites and four doubles, but the entire castle is available for rental, making it the perfect spot for family or group gatherings of up to twenty people. Plenty of common areas encourage both public and private interaction, and include three sitting rooms, a reading room with Internet access, a bar room with fireplace, and a television room. Outside, a lovely pool with adjacent Jacuzzi welcomes guests during the warm months, and the nearby Il Calidario hot springs and wellness center offers Ayurvedic and Shiatsu massages and foot and hand reflexology treatments. You may also immerse yourself in the history and culture of the region with a wine and olive mill tour in the nearby medieval town of Bolgheri. For offshore explorations, embark on a private boat trip to the Tuscan islands of Elba, Giglio, and Giannutri. Mealtime at the castle is always a delightful experience. Since the castle supports its own olive groves and an organic farm, you can be sure its Tuscan dishes are crafted with nothing less than the best, most seasonal ingredients available. With this region also being prime wine-growing country, the dining room offers guests an exceptional opportunity to taste the vintages of local producers like Sassicaia, Ornellaia, Grattamacco, and Petra.

FINE POINTS

Our Family Loved Most: Relaxing in the Jacuzzi by the pool, which overlooks a terraced olive grove.
Rooms: 10 rooms accommodating 20 people; 5 double rooms; 5 suites; and a superior suite. Weekly rentals are preferable during the summer.
Food: Restaurant serving breakfast, lunch, and dinner using fresh, seasonal ingredients from the castle's olive groves and farm.
Suggested Age for Kids: All ages.
Special Features: Outdoor swimming pool and Jacuzzi; exercise equipment; Il Calidario hot springs and wellness center; tours to local wineries and olive mills; boat trips and fishing excursions; guided trips to Siena, Pisa, Lucca, Florence, Volterra, and San Gimignano; sports center with tennis nearby; golf at Il Pelagone golf club 30 minutes away; tickets booked to Siena's Palio; horseback riding trips booked at nearby Parco dell' Uccellina.

CASTELLO DI VICARELLO

Località Vicarello 1 | 58044 Poggi del Sasso - Cinigiano (Grosseto), Italy
Tel. +39 0564990718 | Fax: +39 0564990718
E-mail: info@vicarello.it | Web site: www.castellodivicarello.com | Member of: www.abitarelastoria.it

Exclusive Luxury Family Offer: THE SOUND OF SILENCE: Two nights with breakfast in Giardino Segreto or I Sprone suites; dinner for 2 (beverages not included); 1 massage per person; 1 bottle of wine; 2-night minimum stay. Valid upon availability all year round from €720 per night. Please reference at time of reservation: LFHR-09.

CASTELLO DI VICARELLO is located in Maremma, one of the most captivating areas of the Tuscan countryside, just a short distance from the seacoast, Grosseto, and the hilltop towns of Montalcino, Pienza, and the medieval city of Siena. This enchanting castle dates back to the 12th century, and has undergone an all-embracing restoration involving both the castle and gardens of the extensive medieval estate. Nowadays, Vicarello is a luxurious residence of high style providing personalized service for an exclusive clientele. The décor is refined with a superb intermingling of contemporary furnishings and rare antiques. Four suites and one villa for two to six people are available for guests. Two swimming pools, one of which is an infinity pool, are situated in the gardens, offering breathtaking views of Tuscany's quintessential countryside amid olive groves, vineyards, and woodlands. Owners Aurora and Carlo Baccheschi Berti's combined ingenuity has brought forth a magical place for an ideal family holiday. Currently they are completing a new building with a spa seated in a great spot and offering the same views as the infinity pool inclusive of a sauna, Turkish steam bath, Zen space for yoga or meditation, one massage room, and a great terrace with a wooden hot tub. Upon request, they prepare meals based on local recipes, using products from the castle's vegetable garden and their wonderful extra-virgin organic olive oil. The wine list features vintages from the best of Tuscan wine producers, including Carlo's own superb organic wine for which he received 94 points and 3 blue stars with Castello di Vicarello's cabernet blend, and 91 points and 3 red stars with Terre di Vico, the Sangiovese merlot.

FINE POINTS

Our Family Loved Most: The impeccable Zen-like interior design and infinity pool that provide a feeling of harmony with the surroundings.
Rooms: 4 suites and one villa.
Food: Restaurant by request, featuring authentic cuisine of the Maremma.
Suggested Ages for Kids: All ages.
Special Features: 2 swimming pools; spa with sauna and Turkish steam bath; Zen space for yoga or meditation; massage; hot tub; trekking: unforgettable nature walks in the Mediterranean woods surrounding the castle; horseback riding from nearby stables, which offer a variety of trips exploring the surrounding countryside; golf 50 to 60 minutes away; cooking lessons and wine tasting on request; hunting on request.

CASTELLO ORSINI HOTEL

Via Aldo Bigelli snc | 00017 Nerola | Rome, Italy
Tel. +39 0774683272 | Fax: +39 0774683107
Email: direzione@castelloorsini.it | Web site: www.castelloorsini.it

Exclusive Luxury Family Offer: 1 night in superior double room plus upgrade in suite upon availability plus 1 candlelight dinner (beverage not included) plus use of swimming pool, the fitness center, and open-air fitness track. Also receive 10 percent discount on beauty treatments plus 1 aqua massage or 1 bottle of sparkling wine upon arrival. From €300. Please reference at time of reservation: LFHR-09.

CASTELLO ORSINI HOTEL is located near the Via Salaria 45 km by car north of Rome—but its atmosphere is centuries away in time. Although not lavish in style or décor, travelers desiring a historic immersion into bygone days will delight in this truly authentic medieval experience. From its majestic hillside locale overlooking the verdant Sabina countryside and Lucretili Mountains, this well-preserved property vividly reflects life as it was in a medieval Italian castle. The entrance to the property is certainly a dramatic one, winding through the alleyways of the ancient village below and across the drawbridge of the massive, 10th-century fortress that looks much as it did when it was built as a bulwark against invading Saracens and Hungarians. Today, however, everyone is welcome within its walls. Carefully restored as a monument of living history, the castle serves as a special venue for cultural events, artistic performances, meetings, family gatherings, and celebrations of all kinds. This property encourages hours of exploration, from the fully decorated halls complete with period antiques, furnishings, linens, weaponry, artwork, and frescoes to the beautiful gardens with their fountains and ancient statuary to the panoramic views from the outdoor swimming pool. If all that isn't relaxing enough, the on-site Beauty Center offers a variety of restorative treatments designed to rejuvenate and beautify. At the end of the day, share your experiences over dinner at Castello Orsini's restaurant. Located in the ancient kitchen, it offers regional cuisine and Italian wines. The Castle has two other dining areas located in what were the Knights Hall and the Ancient Orsini Chapel, accommodating large functions of up to 140 people.

FINE POINTS

Our Family Loved Most: Its authentic representation of life as it was in a medieval Italian castle.
Rooms: 51 rooms (suites, junior suites, superior).
Food: 1 restaurant located in the Ancient Kitchen, 2 catering areas located in the Knights Hall and the Ancient Orsini Chapel, which combined can accommodate up to 140 people.
Suggested Ages for Kids: All ages.
Special Features: Year-round swimming pool that's open in summer, sheltered in winter; fitness center; running track; Beauty Center featuring various hydrotherapies, massages, tanning treatments, and facials; steam bath; 3 meeting rooms with up to 180 seats; meetings and special events; laundry service; private, guarded parking with over 200 spaces.

EREMO DELLE GRAZIE

Loc. Monteluco 13 - 06049 | Spoleto (PG), Italy

Tel. +39 074349624 | Fax: +39 074349650

E-mail: eremodellegrazie@tin.it | Web site: www.eremodellegrazie.it | Member of: www.abitarelastoria.it

Exclusive Luxury Family Offer: 10 percent discount applicable to final room rate with a minimum stay of 3 nights. Wherever possible, will apply a room upgrade on all suites. Please reference at time of reservation: LFHR-09.

EREMO DELLE GRAZIE is perched magnificently high above Spoleto on the road to Monteluco in an ancient mountaintop monastery that has given respite to many notable historical figures. Saint Isac and his followers founded it at the beginning of the fifth century after fleeing persecution in their native Syria. Here, they established the Congregation of Hermit Fathers of Monteluco, turning the entire mountaintop into a monastery and place of quiet contemplation. In 1556 Michelangelo wrote in a letter to Vasri of having experienced great pleasure here, "because only in the woods is there peace." It is a recurring phrase at Eremo delle Grazie. Today, it retains its historic qualities of hushed reverence, making it the perfect spot for individuals and couples seeking solace and for groups or families hosting reunions or retreats. The rooms, eleven former monks' cells, are simply outfitted with period furnishings and linens. For more elegant accommodations, we recommend booking the Il Cardinale room. Still, none have air conditioning or televisions. And that's the point. Travelers visit for Eremo's historic and artistic heritage, as well as its famed restaurant, with its superb Umbrian dishes and breakfast buffet, which in the warm months is served outside on the scenic terrace accompanied by panoramic views. Although this remote location requires a car, it is only 4.2 km from Spoleto and within easy reach to surrounding sights. On site, you can relax poolside or explore the natural wonders in the surrounding woods. Indoors, enjoy paintings executed by Ginesio del Barba di Massa in the anteroom, painted wood panels in the library, and the ancient grotto, which today serves as the wine cellar.

FINE POINTS

Our Family Loved Most: The cuisine is the ultimate part of this experience along with the most incredible views of Umbria.
Rooms: 11 rooms.
Food: Breakfast buffet; bar; restaurant.
Suggested Ages for Kids: All ages.
Special Features: Magnificent terrace which can host events for up to 150 people; meeting room can host up to 70 people; complimentary breakfast buffet; mountain biking, tennis, hiking, and rafting in Valnerina all nearby; day excursions into nearby "cities of art," Assisi, Perugia, and Orvieto; visits to nearby wineries and olive oil mills.

HOTEL DEI MELLINI

Via Muzio Clementi 81 00193 | Rome, Italy

Tel. +39 06324771 | Fax: +39 0632477801

E-mail: info@hotelmellini.com | Web site: www.hotelmellini.com

Exclusive Luxury Family Offer: One complimentary drink per person during your stay at the Mellini Bar, along with an upgrade from a double superior to double deluxe room upon availability. Please inform us at time of reservation. Please reference at time of reservation: LFHR-09.

HOTEL DEI MELLINI has provided guests the finest in European-style hospitality since it first opened in 1995, the result of a careful remodeling and interconnection of twin 19th-century townhomes. It is considered Rome's hotel of choice with travelers-in-the-know, including fashion industry professionals, European royalty, and movie stars. No surprise, then, that in 2005 TripAdvisor awarded Hotel Dei Mellini "Best Luxury Hotel in Rome." Every detail, large and small, contributes to the overall feeling of refinement and grace. The hotel's neo-Classical exterior fronts a chic, modern interior whose lobby is decorated with a mix of Italian marbles, crystal chandeliers, Art Deco accents, and a collection of contemporary artwork. The spacious rooms and suites reflect a similar décor, and those on the sixth floor offer views over the rooftops of Rome with St. Peter's dome in the background.

Breakfast is served daily in the hotel's cafeteria where, come summertime, you can sit outside on the patio amid brightly colored bougainvillea. It's the perfect way to start a day of sightseeing or shopping. Hotel Dei Mellini is located on the Tiber's right bank close to the Vatican and St. Peter's Cathedral and is only a short walk from the Spanish Steps, the Trevi Fountain, the Pantheon, and Piazza Navona. The nearby subway station and bus line provide quick access to all other points in the Eternal City. For lunch or dinner, seek out one of the many nearby restaurants. You can tell by the clientele—local residents rather than the touristy crowd—that the food is exceptional and authentic. During the summer, end your day at the rooftop garden with a cocktail or glass of wine. Not only does it have stunning views, but there is also a very private solarium with showers and towels.

FINE POINTS

What Our Family Loved Most: Taking a long moment of quiet contemplation after a busy day by relaxing at the serene rooftop solarium.
Rooms: 80 rooms – single, double, triple, junior suite.
Food: Bar and lounge; breakfast in café; roof garden for cocktails; excellent restaurants nearby.
Suggested Age for Kids: All ages.
Special Features: Handicapped access; 24-hour reception; meeting rooms with state-of-the-art equipment; Wi-Fi, Internet, and e-mail services; rooftop garden and terrace; solarium; laundry service; babysitting; private garage; rollaway beds upon request; city tours; car rental with driver; pick-up service from and to Fiumicino or Clampino airport upon request.

HOTEL EDEN

Via Ludovisi, 49, 00187 | Rome, Italy
Tel. +39 06478121 | Fax: +39 064821584
E-mail: 1872.concierge@lemeridien.com | Web site: www.lemeridien.com/eden

HOTEL EDEN is a Roman landmark set in the heart of the Eternal City and located just off the Via Veneto overlooking the Borghese Gardens. From the moment the doorman greets you, takes your bags, and guides you to check-in, you know all your needs will be graciously met. Perhaps that is why Hotel Eden is a favorite with celebrities past and present and why it has continued to win top industry accolades, including being awarded the Prix Villegiature for Best Hotel in Europe in 2007. Six stories high and overlooking Rome's seven hills, the hotel's top floor rooms offer panoramic views of the city. All are luxurious and spacious, but the Penthouse Suite deserves special mention, with its large terrace, private library, and on-call butler service. Although sophisticated and state-of-the-art, the hotel also boasts a family friendliness typical to Italian hospitality—everything from an extra bed to a special child's menu is available to accommodate those traveling with children. The concierge service is nothing less than superb in every other aspect as well, and the staff is always at the ready to advise on everything from how to avoid long lines at local attractions to booking city tours, rental cars, and tickets to sporting events. The hotel is also within walking distance to the Spanish Steps and the world-class shopping that borders its streets, the haute couture shops of the Via Condotti, and many wonderful cafes and restaurants. Make sure you eat at least once at the hotel's exceptional dining spot, La Terrazza dell' Eden, which offers beautifully prepared international and regional cuisine, a connoisseur's wine list, and one of the most renowned panoramas in the world from its rooftop location.

FINE POINTS

Our Family Loved Most: The lively atmosphere at the rooftop La Terrazza piano bar, where you are a stranger for only about a minute and where, at night, the neighboring buildings are illuminated for a spectacular light show.
Rooms: 108 rooms; 13 suites; 1 penthouse suite.
Food: La Terrazza rooftop bar and restaurant.
Suggested Age for Kids: All ages.
Special Features: 24-hour room service; meeting facilities for 70 people; fitness and spa; cleaning and laundry service; currency exchange; valet parking; special tours booked by concierge, including private tours of the Sistine Chapel, tickets to soccer or rugby matches, and excursions through famed historical sites by horse-drawn carriage.

HOTEL LORD BYRON

Via Giuseppe De Notaris, 5 | 00197 Rome, Italy
Tel. +39 063220404 | Fax: +39 063220405
E-mail: info@lordbyronhotel.com | Web site: www.lordbyronhotel.com

Exclusive Luxury Family Offer: *Rome With Kids*: Accommodation in double room deluxe, junior suite, or suite with extra bed for child (max 14 years old, in room with parents); daily buffet breakfast; 1 child gift bag including a disposable camera, coloring book, crayons, and sweets; three entry tickets to the Explora Children's Museum of Rome (closed Mondays), a little play town with hands-on experiences and experimentation under the watchful eyes of the museum's guides. Rates from €398 per room per day + 10 percent VAT, child free of charge, and minimum two-night stay. Promotion subject to hotel availability. Please reference at time of reservation: LFHR-09.

HOTEL LORD BYRON is located in the Parioli Quarter, one of Rome's most exclusive areas and boasting the city's highest concentration of foreign embassies, multinational corporations, and banks. The Parioli Quarter is also home to a wealth of fine art and greenery. The hotel itself is within walking distance to Borghese Gardens, Via Veneto, the Spanish Steps, and Trevi Fountain. The interior décor is distinctly posh, reflecting the aristocratic heritage of this former town home estate. The staff is as refined as their surroundings and are attentive to your every whim. The guestrooms are decorated in thirties-style Art Deco, while the suites radiate warmth and intimacy. Each room conveys its individual chic allure with unique accents of extensive mirrors, extravagant beds, vintage marble baths, or views over stately villas and the pristine park. This prestigious part of Rome offers so much that many sightseers miss when they opt for more known areas: Palazzo Barberini, National Gallery of Modern Art, Etruscan Museum of Villa Giulia, and Auditorium Parco della Musica. Families travelling with small children will not have to venture far for a visit to the city zoo, Bioparco di Roma. We dine in Rome frequently, but the hotel's restaurant, Sapori del Lord Byron, still remains one of our most memorable family experiences. Their creative menu features a variety of regional dishes presented in mesmerizing Art Nouveau designs, paired with top wines from famous Italian and foreign regions, as well as those of small local producers. This attention to quality and detail earned the restaurant a prestigious "Award of Excellence" by *Wine Spectator* magazine in 2007. The hotel's Il Salotto Lounge & Wine Bar is the perfect finale to a day in the Eternal City.

FINE POINTS

Our Family Loved Most: The intimate atmosphere that permitted our family to reside as though we were in our own home while being thoughtfully looked after.
Rooms: 32 rooms: Double room classic, double room deluxe, junior suite, and suite. Non-smoking accommodations available.
Food: Sapori del Lord Byron restaurant offers unique regional dishes and select Italian wines.
Suggested Ages for Kids: 12 years and up.
Special Features: 24-hour concierge service; multilingual staff; WI-FI Internet throughout hotel; limousine transfer from/to airport/train station (on request); courtesy shuttle service to the city center/Via Veneto, Piazza del Popolo, Spanish Steps, and Via Condotti; in-room dining; same-day laundry and dry-cleaning service (except Sundays); babysitting by prior arrangement; private excursions organized (on request); elevator; money exchange; tourist information; valet parking service; individual climate control; luxury bathrobes and slippers.

HOTEL PALAZZO BOCCI

Via Cavour, 17 | 06038 Spello (PG), Italy
Tel. +39 0742301021 | Fax: +39 0742301464
E-mail: info@palazzobocci.com | Web site: www.palazzobocci.com

Exclusive Luxury Family Offer: 10 percent discount applicable to stays of minimum three nights or more; fruit basket and a bottle of Italian sparkling wine in room upon arrival. Please reference at time of reservation: LFHR-09.

HOTEL PALAZZO BOCCI is positioned in the center of the charming town of Spello, one of the "pearls" of Italy's Middle Ages and also one of the Umbrian towns least crowded with tourists. Built in the 17th century and established as a hotel after meticulous restoration in 1992, Hotel Palazzo Bocci seamlessly blends history, tradition, and fine artwork with the latest in high-tech hospitality. Its fountain entrance, hanging gardens, spectacular Hall of Frescoes, and elegant rooms adorned with wooden beams, classic textiles, and frescoes all combine to create an atmosphere of refined beauty. Located near the center of town, it is also the perfect base from which to explore Spello and the nearby towns of Assisi and Perugia. Established as a Roman colony in the 1st century B.C., Spello bloomed in the early Middle Ages and is a marvel of that era's art and architecture. Of special note is its wealth of churches, many of them bearing artistic treasures such as the frescoes of Pinturicchio in the Baglioni Chapel in Santa Maria Maggiore. Rich in folkloric traditions as well, it is renowned for its *Infiorata*, the night of work spent creating the magnificent carpet of flowers for the Corpus Domini feast, and olive oil and bruschetta fair held each year in May. Spello is also dotted with many lovely shops and galleries selling traditional Umbrian arts and crafts and foodstuffs. Once back at the hotel, you can unwind from your explorations and share your discoveries with a drink in the bar or out on the lovely rooftop terrace. Owned by the same family, Il Molino across the street is considered the official hotel restaurant, and it features the warmth of service and quality of cuisine that typifies the Umbrian region.

FINE POINTS

Our Family Loved Most: Enchanting accommodations coupled by the authentic yet novel Umbrian cuisine of Il Molino.
Rooms: 23 rooms with private baths; 13 double rooms with shower; 2 doubles with bathtub; 2 singles with shower; 6 suites with whirlpool tub.
Suggested Ages for Kids: All ages.
Food: Breakfast; two nearby *enotecas* (wine stores) on the same street that sell Italian wines including the local Montefalco as well as a selection of wonderful local cheeses and prosciuttos; Il Molino restaurant across the street (see restaurant reviews).
Special Features: All rooms are soundproofed and air-conditioned and feature hairdryer, telephone with direct line, color satellite TV, mini-bar and safe; high-speed Internet; reading lounge; bar/lounge; rooftop terrace; hanging garden; pets allowed.

RISTORANTE IL MOLINO

Piazza Matteotti, 6/7 | 06038 - Spello (PG)
Tel. +39 0742651305 | Fax: +39 0742302235
E-mail: ristoranteilmolino@libero.it

> Ristorante Il Molino, like the charming town in which it's situated, is one of the region's best-kept secrets. Exuding rustic elegance and warmth, Il Molino is neither touristy nor pretentious; instead it focuses on promoting nothing less than the fine art and craft of Umbrian cooking.

As Italy's only landlocked region, Umbria is known as Italy's "green heart," an area of gently rolling hills with a sprinkling of rugged countryside that supports an abundance of fertile soil, fish, and wild game. Located across the street from the esteemed Hotel Palazzo Bocci and under the same ownership, Il Molino specializes in creating sophisticated, exquisitely flavored dishes that highlight Umbria's particular gastronomic delights: top-quality olive oil, black truffles, mushrooms, wild asparagus, Norcia salami, farro grain, lentils, grilled meats, game birds, chocolate, and honey. Start with an appetizer of risina, a tiny white bean exclusive to Umbria. Pastas run from the delicately sauced to the rich and robust, and the meats and fish are nothing less than first rate, whether grilled or sautéed and topped with a signature sauce. For dessert, don't miss the dark chocolate tureen with orange cream. Everything is accompanied by a wide range of some of the region's finest wines, including Umbrian classics like red Sagrantino from Montefalco and Rubesco, other distinguished reds from Torgiano, and good white wines from Grechetto and Orvieto, as well as Vin Santo. Located in a 14th-century building originally used as an oil press, the arched dining room offers views of walls from the Roman period and features a magnificent open fireplace that that contributes to the room's intimacy and warmth. The inside dining room seats around one hundred people, but we were fortunate to take pleasure in our meal out on the terrace during a beautiful summer afternoon.

HOTEL REGENCY

Piazza M. D'Azeglio, 3 | 50121 Florence, Italy
Tel. +39 055245247 | Fax: +39 0552346735
E-mail: info@regency-hotel.com | Web site: www.regency-hotel.com

Exclusive Luxury Family Offer: FLORENCE WITH KIDS: Accommodation in double room deluxe, junior suite, or suite with extra bed for child (max. 14 years old, in room with parents); daily buffet breakfast; one child gift bag to include a disposable camera, coloring book, crayons, and sweets; three entry tickets to the Leonardo da Vinci Museum of Florence, featuring an incredible collection of da Vinci's drawings and models made from those drawings. Price: from €398 per room per day + 10 percent VAT; child free of charge minimum 2-night stay; promotion subject to hotel availability. Please reference at time of reservation: LFHR-09.

HOTEL REGENCY is a true European boutique hotel located in the very heart of Florence within close proximity to all the city's main monuments and attractions. You will be welcomed into a delightful haven where refined Florentine qualities and philosophy remain untouched by time. Hotel Regency embodies the ideal home away from home for aficionados of luxury experiences in an atmosphere of long-gone days when ladies and gentlemen traveled in their Sunday best and vintage hospitality was the standard. Every monument, street, and church, regardless of its architectural style and period, reflects the graceful refinement of everyday life in this awe-inspiring city. The hotel's concierge is always on hand to offer touring suggestions and to schedule private chauffeur services or multilingual walking guides. The décor is that of soft Tuscan tones, fine draperies, Renaissance art, elegant antique furnishings, common areas with a living room–like air, and a lovely city garden, which furthers the private-estate ambience of this small but grand hotel. Each guestroom and suite is exquisitely furnished to replicate the charming, hospitable mood of a classic Florentine villa. The hotel's world-renowned restaurant, Relais Le Jardin, serves exquisite gourmet meals, either in the main dining room amid grandiose mirrors, elaborately carved wood panels, and antique, hand-painted stained glass, or in the picturesque veranda overlooking a surreal garden. Weather permitting, this garden is perfect for family gatherings over breakfast or a candlelight dinner, or simply relax with a book in the beauty of the private setting. Dishes are sensationally combined, blending the strong flavors of traditional Tuscan cuisine with a sophisticated flair, always distinctly Italian and carefully matched with rare wines selected by the experienced sommelier.

FINE POINTS

Our Family Loved Most: The luxury of dining in a peaceful, private garden in the center of Florence.
Rooms: 35 rooms: double room classic; double room deluxe; junior suite; suite. Non-smoking accommodations available.
Food: Relais Le Jardin, where Chef Rino Pennucci demonstrates his outstanding ability to craft a robust cuisine based on signature Tuscan flavors.
Suggested Ages for Kids: 12 years and up.
Special Features: 24-hour concierge service; multilingual staff; Wi-Fi Internet throughout hotel; limousine transfer from/to airport/train station upon request; in-room dining; same-day laundry and dry-cleaning service (except Sundays); babysitting by prior arrangement; private excursions organized upon request; private garden; elevator; money exchange; tourist information; valet parking; individual climate control; Carrera marble bathrooms; luxury bathrobes and slippers.

IL BORRO

52040 San Giustino, Valdarno | Tuscany, Italy
Tel. +39 055977053 | Fax: +39 055977055
E-mail: ilborro@ilborro.it | Web site: www.ilborro.com

Exclusive Luxury Family Offer: TUSCAN FAMILY ESCAPE: 2 nights at Il Borro in an apartment housing up to 4 people; 1 dinner for 4 (not including beverages); and wine tour and tasting for 4. Also includes one of the following activities for 4: horseback riding excursion, use of driving range, or use of tennis courts. 2 night minimum stay. Valid upon availability year round, from €530 per night. Please reference at time of reservation: LFHR-09.

IL BORRO comprises two thousand acres of a former 11th-century medieval village that sits in the center of a triangle formed by Arezzo, Florence, and Siena. In the early 1990s, the Ferragamo family purchased the property and began its meticulous restoration into a luxury vacation spot for discerning travelers. The family brings to Il Borro the same quality and attention to detail that make them a world-renowned name in fashion. The aim is to allow visitors to experience the feeling of Tuscan life as it has been led for centuries, while at the same time enjoying state-of-the art service and amenities. Accommodations are available at farmhouses, villas, and apartments, each of which are outfitted with modern kitchens, refrigerator/freezers, dishwashers, dishes and utensils, washing machines, and fully outfitted bathrooms. The secret of the whole restoration is the strict respect of the traditional Tuscany style. The best way to experience the beauty of this estate is to set out on foot and start exploring. The property includes a lovely church, shops selling local wares, olive groves, and a winery that offers tasting and tours. You can also book an excursion to a nearby city—Florence, Siena, Arezzo, Pisa, and many others are all easy day trips. The staff will be happy to help you plan, point out the best shopping areas, and suggest places "off the beaten track." When it comes to dining, you can cook, have meals prepared and delivered, or go to the village and dine at L'Osteria del Borro, which offers elegant Tuscan dishes prepared from locally grown ingredients and extra-virgin olive oil produced from Il Borro's five thousand olive trees. The estate also grows five varieties of grapes to produce four distinctive wines: the reds, Il Borro, Pian di Nova, and Polissena; and one white, Lamelle, which you can order at dinner as well.

FINE POINTS

Our Family Loved Most: Immersing ourselves in the daily rhythms of rural Tuscan life and experiencing through the wine, olive oil, and food the wonderful bounty of this land.
Rooms: 12 apartments in the medieval village, 4 farmhouses in the countryside and 2 villas.
Food: Self-catering; dining in the nearby village at L'Osteria del Borro.
Suggested Age for Kids: All ages.
Special Features: Welcome information packet with important local phone numbers and list of recommended restaurants, museums, and galleries; maid service; babysitting; swimming pool; host of activities including winery tours, arts and crafts classes, mountain biking, hot air ballooning, horseback riding, hunting (depending on the season), and golfing; cooking lessons; wine tasting and tours; day trips and excursions planned; on-site Artisans Mall—seven shops featuring local arts and crafts, including David and Massimo jewelry, Maddalena ceramics and glassware, handmade shoes, tasteful gifts, and original items for the home.

LUCIGNANELLO BANDINI

Localita Lucignano d'Asso | 53020 San Giovanni d'Asso - Siena
Tel. +39 0577803068 | Fax: +39 0577803082 | P. Iva 00169080520
E-mail: info@borgolucignanello.com | Web site: www.borgolucignanello.com | Member of: www.abitarelastoria.it

Exclusive Luxury Family Offer: FREE OLIVE OIL TASTING WITH SOMMELIER PLUS: All guests receive a welcome basket with wine, olive oil, and breakfast products. 10 percent off for stays of two weeks. Please reference at time of reservation: LFHR-09.

LUCIGNANELLO BANDINI comprises five two-bedroom houses and a five-bedroom farmhouse located in the hilltop hamlet of Lucignano d'Asso in the southernmost tip of Tuscany about a half hour's drive from Siena. Owned by the Piccolomini family since the 15th century, the hamlet epitomizes Tuscan country charm with its gold and rose-hued stone, two churches, quaint piazzas, vineyards and olive groves, and breathtaking views overlooking the Orcia Valley and the Crete Senesi. Here, daily life is still informed by long-established agricultural traditions and the harmonious relationship between civil society and the environment. One of Italy's foremost restoration experts, Paolo Alberto Rossi, certainly stayed true to those traditions when he renovated the property in the 1990s. Each house reflects the interplay between interior and exterior, natural and manmade. Elegant furnishings and accessories beautifully balance texture and tone: the pale-beige of local travertine, warm terracotta hues, seasoned wood, trompe-l'oeil motifs, hand-painted ceramics, jacquard textiles, and bright cottons. Even the swimming pools meld seamlessly with their surroundings. There's no traffic in the hamlet, but guests can rent scooters on which to explore its streets and those of neighboring villages like Montalcino and Montepulciano. Florence, Lucca, Pisa, Siena, and San Gimignano are easily reached within a few hours or less by car. Breakfast is available, but otherwise the property is geared toward self-catering. Everything needed to eat simply but well is provided at the local store and at the alimentary at the farmhouse: fresh cheese, prosciutto, vegetables, fruit, bread, pastas, and local wines. Notable nearby restaurants include Montalcino's Trattoria Sciame with its wonderful wild boar, and Montepulciano's La Grotta, renowned for its duck pasta and Vino Nobile di Montepulciano, one of the great Tuscan wines.

FINE POINTS

Our Family Loved Most: Spectacular views from the hillside infinity pool. On-site "olive store" where you can purchase award-winning cold-pressed extra-virgin olive oil made from olives grown on the family property.

Rooms: Four of the houses, Casa Amadeo, Casa Remo, Casa Clemintina, and Casa Severino, sleep 4–6; Casa Maria, the "honeymoon suite," is recommended for 2 persons, but will sleep 3; the Casale Sarageto farmhouse sleeps up to 8.

Food: Small store inside the farmhouse sells local olive oils and other products; osteria serving light snacks; country store in the hamlet.

Suggested Ages for Kids: 8 and up.

Special Features: Infinity swimming pool; scooter and mountain bike rentals; business services to include computer, photocopier, and fax machine; laundry and iron service; informal cooking classes by local housewives; hunting and mushroom gathering expeditions in winter; small pets welcome.

PALAZZO VIVIANI

HOTELPHILOSOPHY

Castello di Montegridolfo V. | Roma, 38 47837 Montegridolfo (RN), Italy

Tel. +39 0541855350

Email: montegridolfo@mobygest.it | Web site: www.hotelphilosophy.net

Exclusive Luxury Family Offer: Complimentary fruit basket and *Dolcetti* (local biscuits typical of area) in room upon arrival. Please reference at time of reservation: LFHR-09.

PALAZZO VIVIANI of Castello di Montegridolfo is located a few kilometers inland of the Adriatic Sea, on the borders of The Emilia-Romagna and Marche regions—two areas not as well known as Tuscany, yet just as superb. On approach by car, the private hilltop village's prominent gate tower is visibly situated among a countryside dotted with abandoned fortresses, towers, ancient churches, and small historical sites. Castello di Montegridolfo is three hotels in one. Each of the eight elegant rooms of the aristocratic manor house, Palazzo Viviani, is lavishly decorated, all with a variety of antiques and some with restored frescos on the ceilings and walls. All offer wonderful views. Located beside the swimming pool, Casa del Pittore is a more discreet structure with seven romantic rooms offering comfort in a unique yet charming style. The eight suites of Borgo Antico and thirty rooms and suites of Borgo Nuovo Suites are the perfect blend of absolute privacy and maximum comfort, and some provide small kitchens. The impeccable renovation and maintenance of Montegridolfo create an authentic, comfortable, and luxurious escape that assures the phrase "this is Italy" accompanies every sensation. Some of the best of these sensations are the tastes of Il Ristoro in the Palazzo Viviani, one of Montegridolfo's three outstanding restaurants. A highly sophisticated tasting menu, which changes daily, incorporates a plethora of local *ingredienti tipici*, including truffles and the famous Formaggio della Fossa, into eight or so perfectly mastered courses. At the Osteria dell'Accademia, enjoy traditional local dishes while sitting on a terrace with a sea view, or try wood oven specialties of the Grotta dei Gridolfi, open all year. In the summer months, sit out in the Piazzetta at the Ritrovo del Vecchio Forno.

FINE POINTS

Our Family Loved Most: Exquisite modernization of an authentic ancient village.
Rooms: 53 total: 8 at Palazzo Viviani; 7 at Casa del Pittore; 8 at Borgo Antico; and 30 at Borgo Nuoco.
Food: Il Ristoro; Osteria dell'Accademia; Grotta dei Gridolfi.
Suggested Ages for Kids: All ages.
Special Features: Near Adriatic Sea; garden/terrace; ideal for weddings; mountain biking rentals; wine tasting; culinary tastings; excursions and tours; jogging track; wheelchair accessible elevator; 400-seat modern meeting center for workshops and conferences.

PARK HOTEL VILLA GRAZIOLI

Via Umberto Pavoni, 19 | 00046 Grottaferrata (Rome), Italy

Tel. +39 069454001 | Fax: +39 069413506

E-mail: info@villagrazioli.com | Web site: www.villagrazioli.com

Exclusive Luxury Family Offer: One free candlelight dinner for 2 persons (3 courses including local wine) for a minimum 3-night stay in a double room. Please reference at time of reservation: LFHR-09.

PARK HOTEL VILLA GRAZIOLI sits majestically on the outskirts of Rome at the foot of Tusculum Hill just outside Frascati. Its locale showcases expansive views of the surrounding urban areas, as well the Tyrrhenian Sea, whose surface glistens like a polished sheet of glass in the distance. Once a meeting place for artists, poets, architects, and other famous personalities, including the Marquis de Sade (who describes the house in his writings as one of the most elegant in the region), this 16th-century masterpiece was eventually abandoned. Rescued from complete neglect in 1987 by the Company Villa Grazioli, the property underwent a thorough restoration of its architecture, decor, and fifteen-thousand-square-foot park and gardens. Today, this Italian National Monument is also a fifty-eight-room hotel that provides architecture and history buffs with a fascinating ambience while at the same time serving as a comfortable and stylish retreat from the urban hustle and bustle. The hotel is noted for its beautifully preserved frescoes, created over three periods, which decorate the floors and ceilings of the main floor, including an entire gallery named after that room's painter, Giovanni Paolo Pannini. It is also famous for the view from its rooftop terrace, which is reached by a spiral staircase in the west wing. While located twenty-one kilometers from Rome, a short train ride from the nearby town of Frascati effortlessly puts you in the thick of the city. The surrounding towns of Frascati and Grottaferatta are also well worth a visit as they feature fine shops and restaurants with authentic local Roman (Lazio-Regional) cuisine. Within the hotel itself, the Acquaviva restaurant complements the refined historic ambience with exquisitely prepared Mediterranean food and the region's most famous and traditional wines.

FINE POINTS

Our Family Loved Most: Dinner outside on the terrace overlooking the twinkling lights of Rome; the absolute luxury during the summer months of a refreshing dip in the pool after a day spent touring Rome.
Rooms: 56 rooms; 2 suites.
Food: Bar; breakfast and lunch; dinner at Acquaviva restaurant.
Suggested Ages for Kids: All ages.
Special Features: Air-conditioned rooms with satellite TV; Wi-Fi throughout entire hotel, purchased by the hour or day; banquet facilities for weddings, cocktail parties, and special events of up to 200 people; parking for up to 120 cars; swimming pool; lush park and gardens; free hourly shuttles to and from the hotel to Frascati train station; special arrangement with the Castel Gandolfo Golf Club (10 km from hotel) and with a wellness center (2 km from hotel) featuring fitness, steam bath, sauna, Jacuzzi, indoor pool, massage, and beauty center.

RELAIS CAMPO REGIO

Via della Sapienza 25 | 53100 Siena, Italy
Tel. +39 0577222073 | Fax: +39 0577237308
E-mail: relais@camporegio.com | Web site: www.camporegio.com | Member of: www.abitarelastoria.it

Exclusive Luxury Family Offer: A GRACIOUS SIENESE WELCOME: 10 percent discount off room rate for stays of 3 nights or more; fruit basket, bottle of wine, and special book regarding the "History of Siena" upon arrival. Please reference at time of reservation: LFHR-09.

RELAIS CAMPO REGIO is a luxury bed and breakfast–style hotel based inside a historic building in the center of Siena, home to the famed Palio horserace. The Via della Sapienza was once the busiest street in medieval Siena, and it remains home to the city's university and the Intronati's academy, whose prestige is still visible today in the famous city library situated adjacent to the hotel. Renovated in 2005, the Relais Campo Regio epitomizes first-class, high-tech service and amenities. Every appointment evokes an aura of old-world hospitality and elegance, from exquisite antiques and fine embroidered linens to plush terry cloth towels and monogrammed bathrobes. The heart of the hotel is its cozy bar, from which many an easy friendship between travelers has been forged. You can also take your aperitif or coffee out onto the hotel's terrace and enjoy breathtaking and expansive views of the city and Campo Regio valley. The hotel is also within walking distance to some of Siena's best shops, restaurants, museums, and points of interest, including the Piazza del Campo, the Museo Civico with its Simone Martini frescos, and the Pinacoteca Nazionale, containing 11th- and 12th-century masterpieces from Siena's golden age of art. Additionally, the picturesque towns of the Sienese countryside, as well as the larger cities of Florence, Pisa, Arezzo, and Lucca, are all nearby. As befitting a high-end boutique bed and breakfast, the morning meal is distinguished by a bountiful continental buffet breakfast served out on the terrace. For lunch or dinner, reception will be happy to recommend a restaurant according to appetite and taste—the neighborhood is dotted with exceptional eateries.

FINE POINTS

Our Family Loved Most: The spectacular views from the terrace.
Rooms: 6 rooms.
Food: Bar, breakfast buffet; numerous wonderful restaurants nearby for lunch and dinner.
Suggested Ages for Kids: 12 years and up.
Special Features: Soundproofed, air conditioned rooms with satellite televisions, mini bars, safes, and telephones; complimentary continental breakfast buffet; parking services upon request; elevator; reading room; shuttle to and from airport by prior arrangement; personalized walking tours and countryside car excursions; Palio tickets booked by prior arrangement or available by purchase from front desk.

RELAIS & CHATEAUX VILLA LA VEDETTA

Viale Michelangiolo, 78 | 50125 Florence (Firenze), Italy
Tel. +39 055681631 | Fax: +39 0556582544
E-mail: info@villalavedettahotel.com | Web site: www.villalavedettahotel.com

Exclusive Luxury Family Offer: Enjoy 1 fine dining experience at Onice Restaurant with a special Luxury Family discount of 20 percent (does not include beverages). Valid all year based on availability when staying at Villa La Vedetta. Please reference at time of reservation: LFHR-09.

RELAIS & CHATEAUX VILLA LA VEDETTA offers magnificent views of Florence from its regal hilltop position high above the Arno on Piazzale Michelangleo and just a few steps from Ponte Vecchio. Neo-Renaissance in design and augmented by Art Deco–style décor, the hotel looks and feels like a gracious countryside retreat, yet it is only a short walk, drive, or shuttle ride to the urban excitement below. Aristocratic and also alluringly romantic, Villa La Vedetta charms with chic, well-appointed rooms, lush gardens, beautiful panoramic swimming pool, large terrace overlooking Florence, and elegant bar and restaurant. Priding itself on accommodating a variety of travelers, the hotel delights in welcoming families with small children, each of whom receives upon arrival a sweet treat, a drawing kit, and a specially designed map of kid-centric sights in Florence. The restaurant also offers a special children's menu that happily accommodates their tastes. With its able staff, scenic grounds, and views at every turn, Relais & Chateaux Villa La Vedetta has become a popular spot for weddings, reunions, and anniversaries—a place where memories are made for a lifetime. It's also a great place to relax after a day spent touring the city. We suggest the following: a dip in the twenty-person Jacuzzi to relax aching muscles, followed by a cocktail or aperitif at the elegant onyx bar, and then dinner at Onice. This splendid dining area with its vaulted ceiling and two large, arched glass doors opening to the garden, swimming pool, and Jacuzzi is known for its skillful fusion of traditional and international flavors to create innovative seasonal menus. Onice has won the interest of authoritative gastronomic critics and earned excellent reviews from prestigious magazines for its fabulous food, impeccable service, and wine list concentrating primarily on important Tuscan reds.

FINE POINTS

Our Family Loved Most: Private rooftop terrace for an intimate dining experience overlooking landscape gardens, pool, and Florence.
Rooms: 18 deluxe rooms and suites.
Food: Pool bar; Onice restaurant and bar.
Suggested Age for Kids: All ages.
Special Features: External panoramic swimming pool with a separate Jacuzzi for 20 people; large terrace overlooking Florence; garden and private park; 24-hour room service and front desk service; sauna and fitness center; meeting and banquet room; full business services; private parking and valet service; non-smoking rooms; laundry and ironing service; babysitting upon request; special services for women traveling alone, small children, and pets; bike rental; shuttle service to city center.

RELAIS LA CORTE DEI PAPI

Via La Dogana, 12 | 52040 | Loc. Pergo di Cortona (Arezzo), Italy
Tel. +39 0575614109 | Fax: +39 0575614963 | Cell: +39 3483264823
E-mail: info@lacortedeipapi.com | Web site: www.lacortedeipapi.com

Exclusive Luxury Family Offer: PLEASURE FOR YOUR EYES BY DAY, EXCITEMENT FOR YOUR PALATE BY NIGHT: 3 night's accommodations; bottle of La Corte dei Papi estate wine and fresh fruit in room upon arrival; lavish buffet breakfast; 3 romantic à la carte dinners; 1/2-day wine tours and tastings with English-speaking guide. Valid upon availability all year round. Price: from €495 total package per person in a deluxe room; third bed free for child up to 12 years of age, otherwise from €40 per person, per day charge applies. Cottages, junior suites, and suites are available upon request. Please reference at time of reservation: LFHR-09.

RELAIS LA CORTE DEI PAPI rests in the heart of Tuscany's rolling hills that border Umbria, within a few minutes from Cortona. This small town of ancient origins has preserved its appeal as an antique medieval village. It's the ideal spot to enjoy a family vacation within a peaceful setting surrounded by nature and near small villages, "cities of art," and breathtaking landscapes. Once an 18th-century historic dwelling and residence of the current owners, the Papi family, it has been skillfully restored using the existing antique materials or utilizing similar ones obtained locally. Today, Relais La Corte dei Papi is a magnificent infusion of superior elegance and charm, reflecting David Papi's passion for providing top fine dining and hospitality experiences. The garden, with a swimming pool and gazebo, are gracefully encompassed by the relais, creating an exclusive setting of pure relaxation. The hotel offers eight different types of accommodations, from guestrooms to spacious junior suites. All are decorated with warm antique furnishings and modern comforts. David Papi appears to be in all places, all the time. He's a Houdini in his own right, showing up at receptions to offer assistance with a day of tours and excursions, poolside to be sure you have sufficient towels or drinks, or even during dinner to pair the perfect wine with your selections. Restaurant La Corte dei Papi's chefs will dazzle you as they prepare Tuscan cuisine with a contemporary touch; fresh pasta, bread, and desserts are all made from scratch. The silverware, the prized porcelain, and delicate Flanders linen unite with first-class service to envelop you in a romantic and luxurious setting.

FINE POINTS

Our Family Loved Most: Personalized service and attentiveness provided by owner David Papi, which truly makes all guests feel right at home.
Rooms: 8 rooms: room/cottage deluxe; junior suite classic and deluxe.
Food: Bar; La Corte dei Papi restaurant, featuring creative and traditional Tuscan cuisine, fusion, vegetarian, and seafood; all open to public.
Suggested Ages for Kids: All ages.
Special Features: Swimming pool; garden; parking; cooking lessons; wine tour; organization of guided tours and excursions; laundry and ironing service; limousine service; car rental.

RESIDENZA DEL MORO

Via del Moro 15 | 50123 Florence, Italy
Tel. +39 055290884 or 055264269 | Fax: +39 0552648494
E-mail: info@residenzadelmoro.com | Web site: www.residenzadelmoro.com

Exclusive Luxury Family Offer: Minimum stay 2 nights in a junior suite; 1 night free in their sister property in Pietrasanta, Albergo Pietrasanta. Valid upon availability all year round. Please reference at time of reservation: LFHR-09.

RESIDENZA DEL MORO is located in the heart of Florence in the *piano nobile* of the beautifully restored 16th-century Palazzo Niccolini-Bourbon. Home to some of Florence's leading aristocrats over five centuries, the palazzo envelops guests in an atmosphere that combines Renaissance, Baroque, Enlightenment, Romantic, and contemporary art and culture. The historic and artistic elements are enhanced by cutting-edge comforts and technologies as well as faultless service at a level superior among Florence's five-star luxury hotels. Manager Barbara Pardini (who also oversees operations at Albergo Pietrasanta) waits on guests as if they were members of her own family, and the hotel's butler service excels at accommodating every need. All eleven suites are gems of refined taste, displaying original frescoes, furniture, antiques, artwork, and silks and brocades from the 15th through 19th centuries. The hotel's Renaissance and Baroque architecture includes its 16th-century façade, 17th-century staircase, and spectacular 15th-century rooftop and garden, a wonderfully romantic spot for sharing a drink from the hotel bar. All the marvels of Florence are mere minutes away: the Church of Santa Maria Novella is two hundred meters up the street, and the Santa Maria del Fiore, the Duomo, Giotto's Campanile, and the Baptistery are five minutes by foot. The Uffizi Gallery is only ten minutes away. While there is no on-site restaurant, the Residenze Del Moro does start your day with a fabulous breakfast. As for lunch and dinner, the knowledgeable staff are more than happy to direct you to their favorite Florentine wine bars and trattorias, which most certainly will include a recommendation to the nearby Trattoria Garga, with its contemporary paintings; Il Latini, featuring old-fashioned family style service; and Buca Lapi, famous for its *Bistecca alla Fiorentina*.

FINE POINTS

Our Family Loved Most: The rooftop garden and the marvelous collection of contemporary Italian artwork.
Rooms: 11 outstanding suites.
Food: Breakfast; bar; tearoom.
Suggested Ages for Kids: All ages.
Special Features: 24-hour reception and room service; 24-hour bar and petite carte service; butler service; all rooms feature: linen sheets, cashmere blankets, bathrooms with tub and shower, customized cosmetic line, mini bar, safe, air conditioning, standard and cordless telephone lines, satellite LCD television, modem connection, plug and play, and Wi-Fi Internet access; gym; private garden; conference room; pets welcomed; babysitter and pet sitter service; garage with valet; cultural tours and day trips by arrangement.

ITALY SEGWAY TOURS

Via de Servi 13, Florence, Italy

Tel./Fax: +39 0552398855

E-mail: info@italysegwaytours.com | Web site: www.italysegwaytours.com

Exclusive Luxury Family Offer: 10 percent off audio guides with tour leader. This service is available for those who would like to hear recorded information but also have the accompanying support of a staff person. Please reference at time of reservation: LFHR-09.

Imagine effortlessly gliding through the streets of Florence, soaking in the city's beauty as you stop to marvel at its most famous monuments and architecture. Imagine learning fascinating facts and lively anecdotes from a guide skilled in the fine art of storytelling. Then imagine doing it all without weary feet, aching knees, or having to emit a single puff of engine exhaust. Thanks to the dynamic, Florence-based company ITALY SEGWAY TOURS, the safe, easy-to-use technology that revolutionized personal transportation is now revolutionizing the tourism industry. By offering the first and only Segway-guided tours of Florence, Italy Segway Tours makes it possible to see the treasures of Florence up close and personal while also helping to prevent further damage to monuments and architecture caused by pollution. Each three-hour tour begins with a thirty-minute orientation session at the company's offices. Once everyone is comfortable with the operation of their personal Segways, the group heads out under the leadership of a professional, multilingual guide who is degreed in both art and history. Each tour is limited to no more than six people, so you're guaranteed an individual and intimate experience. Tours are offered starting at ten o'clock in the morning and three o'clock in the afternoon. In Florence, you'll visit the Porcellino, Piazza della Signoria, the Uffizi-Ponte Vecchio, Santa Crocie, Bargello. Dante's house, Duomo, Battistero, Piazza della Republica, Piazza degli Strozzi, and Tornabuoni. This was one of our most memorable family activities while visiting Italy—wonderfully educational and most definitely a unique, nontraditional way to experience Florence.

RESIDENZA TORRE DI SAN MARTINO

Castello di Rivalta | 29010 Gazzola (Piacenza), Italy
Tel. +39 0523972002 | Fax: +39 0523972030
E-mail: info@torredisanmartino.it | Web site: www.torredisanmartino.it | Member of: www.abitarelastoria.it

Exclusive Luxury Family Offer: FAMILY WEEKEND IN ROMANTIC DELUXE COTTAGES: 1 night in a deluxe cottage with separate room for children; self-catered breakfast; visit to the magnificent Castle of Rivalta. Available weekends year round, except during national and bank holidays. A second night may be added for extra charge. Not included are special area children's activities depending on season: Park of Fables in the Castle of Gropparello; River Park waterslides; Adventure Park of Stoppa. The Residenza can reserve all activities. Price: From €250, 2 adults and 1–2 children €40 per child, per night. Please reference at time of reservation: LFHR-09.

RESIDENZA TORRE DI SAN MARTINO lies in the authentically restored 11th-century village of Rivalta, among the gentle hill country of Piacenza, in the heart of the Trebbia Valley—a welcoming area rich in culture, history, and great food. Here we find a special property where the atmosphere is elegant yet warm, relaxed, and very romantic. The houses in the village were originally craftsmen's workshops and farmers' cottages, which have been transformed since the 1950s into restaurants, bars, a winery, and shops selling locally produced products. The Castle of Rivalta dates back to 218 BC when the battle on Trebbia took place between the Cartaginesi troops of Hannibal and the Roman legions. Still owned by the original Landi family, it towers above the village. Today, its gardens and guesthouse are used for banquets, events, meetings, conferences, and weddings, which may be celebrated in the village's 14th-century church of San Martino. The guestrooms are each uniquely decorated in an upscale manner complete with all modern conveniences. Yet, the property still maintains an atmosphere of bygone times, brought out by the wooden ceilings, beds with baldachins, velvets, and authentic antique furnishings. The building that today houses the Rocchetta restaurant is the oldest in the village, with its 14th-century walls still intact. In the past, this was where the farm animals, horses, and cattle were kept. The restaurant boasts a seasonal menu of meats and seafood, and in the summer *al fresco* dining offers enchanting views of the castle and surrounding valley. For some of the most renowned regional cuisine in Emilia-Romagna, experience Antica Locanda del Falco; do visit its traditional butcher shop and wine cellar with important Italian regional productions plus some foreign wines.

FINE POINTS

Our Family Loved Most: A charming hotel set within a small inclusive village offering fascinating history, with artistic views.
Rooms: 9 deluxe; 1 deluxe junior suite; 6 cottages.
Food: Nearby restaurants Antica Locanda del Falco and La Rocchetta.
Suggested Ages for Kids: All ages.
Special Features: located in medieval village with restaurants, bars, a winery featuring the wines of the Borgo di Rivalta, and shops; tours of Castle of Rivalta; parking; tennis, golf, horseback riding, biking, hiking, rafting, and kayaking all nearby.

ANTICA LOCANDA DEL FALCO

Castello Di Rivalta | Rivalta di Gazzola (Piacenza), Italy
Tel. +39 0523978101 | Fax: +39 0523978331
E-mail: ilfalcodirivalta@libero.it | Web site: locandadelfalco.com

> Antica Locanda Del Falco is located in a 15th-century building that once housed the Hebrew money exchange for the medieval village of Rivalta.

A historical treasure of Emilia-Romagna's Piacenza region, the restaurant has long been a favorite dining spot with the locals, including Piacenza native Giorgio Armani. And it's a good bet that if the locals love it, you'll be in for an exceptional treat. So, if your trip to Italy happens to include a visit to Rivalta, you simply must put this on your agenda. The restaurant has been run since 1975 by members of the Piazza family, who for years worked as highly regarded butchers. That ability to discern the best in fresh and cured meats has served them well in the restaurant. Today, husband-and-wife team Marco and Sabrina Piazza oversee the kitchen, dining room, and wine cellar operations, as well as the adjacent shop selling local wines and foodstuffs. Marco works the front of the house, greeting guests and lending his expert knowledge to their food and wine selections, which include important Italian vintages and some very excellent selections from France. Meanwhile, Sabrina works her magic back in the kitchen, crafting delicious interpretations of Tuscan classics. Her menu is distinguished by the quality of its grilled and salted meat dishes, homemade pastas with accompanying sauces, and decadent desserts. She also receives consistent reviews for her *bruschetta*, proving the Tuscan adage that even the simplest things should be done extraordinarily well. The restaurant is open for both lunch and dinner and seats about one hundred people inside. A handful of tables on a lovely patio provides wonderful *al fresco* dining during the warmer months.

TOMBOLO TALASSO RESORT

Via del Corallo, 3 | 57022 Marina di Castagneto Carducci (Livorno)
Tel. +39 056574530 | Fax: +39 0565744052
E-mail: info@tombolotalasso.it | Web site: www.tombolotalasso.it

Exclusive Luxury Family Offer: A Family Welcome • Fruit basket and a bottle of Italian sparkling wine in room upon arrival. Please reference at time of reservation: LFHR-09.

TOMBOLO TALASSO RESORT is located within a small Mediterranean beach town on the Tuscan coast, seventy-five kilometers south of Pisa and an hour and a half from Florence. This five-star resort is distinguished by its unsurpassed balance of both a peaceful and relaxing atmosphere for adults and close proximity to the sea where families can enjoy the beautiful beach. Each guest is welcomed graciously, and the service aims to satisfy every guest's most personal desires and expectations. All guest rooms are slightly different and of an eclectic décor, creating a chic Mediterranean atmosphere. At the Tombolo Thalassotherapy Center and Spa, guests are pampered with all the treatments necessary to rediscover health, well-being, and harmony. Pure sea water is their unique resource, obtained directly from the source and enabling Tombolo to offer a unique selection of Thalassotherapic treatments like hydro-massages with algae or salts, horizontal sea rain showers, and much more. The food alone is worth the entire journey. Sala Corallo restaurant, with its adjacent wine bar lounge and romantic outdoor terrace overlooking the sea, is the ideal atmosphere to discover the art that is their local cuisine, a fusion of Mediterranean and international flavors. Only the freshest local ingredients are used: olive oil, meat, game, cheese and, of course, fish from the nearby Gulf of Baratti. The magnificent buffet of antipasti and desserts served every night could suffice as a meal alone, but the delicately prepared entrées are memorable and well complimented by the top Italian and international wines from their extensive cellar (about three hundred labels, including the renowned local Bolgheri wines). Tombolo is an ultimate Tuscan getaway amid the serenity of the sea and countryside.

FINE POINTS

Our Family Loved Most: Relaxing in the heavenly waters contained by the grotto, in the five Thalasso pools.
Rooms: 130 rooms and suites with views of the sea or the park.
Food: Sala Corallo restaurant; wine bar and cellar; pool bar.
Suggested Ages for Kids: All ages.
Special Features: Private beach; 5 swimming pools; panoramic terrace; garden; babysitting service; kids menu; kids pool; playroom; spa and wellness center with relaxing healing and beauty treatments, massage, Jacuzzi, Finnish sauna, Turkish/steam bath, and Roman bath; bathrobe and slippers for children; combined treatments for mother and child and treatments for children (on request); meeting/banquet facilities; business center; laundry; Internet; guest parking.

VILLA CAMPESTRI

Via di Campestri 19/22 | 50039 Vicchio di Mugello (Florence), Italy
Tel. +39 0558490107 | Fax: +39 0558490108
E-mail: villa.campestri@villacampestri.it | Web site: www.villacampestri.com | Member of: www.abitarelastoria.it

Exclusive Luxury Family Offer: *A Trip Through the Extra-Virgin Olive Oil Culture*; a delightful, immersed experience of the true essence of olive oil's origin and many uses, plus cooking lessons and tastings; 3 days / 2 nights accommodation superior double room; complimentary upgrade to junior suite based on availability upon arrival; 250 ml bottle of extra-virgin olive oil; 4-course dinner at Villa Campestri's L'Olivaia restaurant (excluding beverages); daily buffet breakfast; cooking course with chef Roberto Zanieri on preparation of typical Tuscan dishes using hotel's extra-virgin olive oil; afternoon olive oil tasting in the *Oleoteca* of Villa Campestri with specialist Paolo Pasquali. Valid upon availability from €590 for 2 people. Please reference at time of reservation: LFHR-09.

VILLA CAMPESTRI is set in a large private park of extraordinary beauty on a hillside facing the Mugello valley, just thirty-five kilometers from Florence. The villa is in the middle of the Tuscan countryside surrounded by a natural landscape of lawns and ancient olive trees, along with shady oak and chestnut woods. A lovely swimming pool is majestically positioned and offers a panoramic view of the valley below against the backdrop of the Apennine Mountain chain and Mount Falterona. The noble Florentine Roti Michelozzi family held ownership of the villa and the surrounding lands for nearly seven hundred years until 1989, when they sold the entire Campestri property to the present owner, Paolo Pasquali. Villa Campestri is an impressive Renaissance house that has been carefully restored into a fine hotel using authentic materials, maintaining the building's original charming appearance. A stay with Paolo and his family is an outstanding culinary delight of the highest degree, as well as a fascinating experience of their notable estate. The first *Oleoteca* (olive oil center) in Italy is located in the villa's cellars; Paolo's personalized tasting courses and tours of the oil press are enthralling. The restaurant offers specialties of Tuscan cuisine accompanied by the finest local and national wines. Their own farm produces the extra-virgin olive oil, vegetables, and most of the fruit organically. Chef Roberto Zanieri and his staff offer a cuisine rooted in tradition with its use of ancient flavors and herbs. Within this gastronomic context there is nevertheless room for creativity, resulting in original recipes comprising utterly delectable flavors. The chocolate fondant with Villa Campestri extra-virgin olive oil heart and silky chocolate is the crema della crema.

FINE POINTS

Our Family Loved Most: The artful mingling of their organic extra-virgin olive oil within all aspects of their cuisine; the "Olive Oil Menu."
Rooms: 25 rooms.
Food: L'Olivaia restaurant, with a wine list featuring both fine Tuscan wines and those from other regions.
Suggested Ages for Kids: All ages.
Special Features: Cooking courses, including an extra-virgin olive oil tasting course; private park of 120 hectares; truffle-hunting; plant your own olive tree; guided tours of the oak and chestnuts woods around the villa or to cultural or historical sites in the Mugello; mountain bike tours.

VILLA DI PIAZZANO

Localita Piazzano, 06069 | Cortona, Italy
Tel. +39 075826226 | Fax: +39 075826336
E-mail: info@villadipiazzano.com | Web site: www.villadipiazzano.com

Exclusive Luxury Family Offer: 10 percent discount on all room rates with a minimum stay of 4 nights. Please reference at time of reservation: LFHR-09.

VILLA DI PIAZZANO is located in the countryside just outside Cortona on the border between Tuscany and Umbria. Reflecting the linear style typical of Italy's early Renaissance, it stands as a symbol of that era's economic and artistic power, when stately manors like this one dotted the country as retreats for the newly prosperous. Villa di Piazzano was built starting in 1464 as the hunting manor of Cardinal Silvio Passerini (the lobby proudly displays the foundation stone) and then later served as a convent and farming estate. It underwent extensive restoration beginning in 1999 and today is classified as a Historical Residence. The Wimpole family, who owns the villa, has a long tradition of excellence in the hospitality industry. Their personal touch is evident throughout the property, making a stay here an immersive experience in Italian hospitality and culture. A walk through the grounds takes you into an ancient garden where the scent of linden trees, jasmine, and Italian oaks, along with wild roses, lavender, and Peonies, perfume the air. The delightful aroma enhances your days spent laying by the pool or under the shade of the century-old oaks. The rooms are airy, spacious, and punctuated with wide windows that open onto magnificent views of the surrounding fields and hills. If nature plays a central role here, so does its bounty. From May to September the staff organizes special wine tastings in the evenings, and during November's olive harvest, guests may watch as the fruit is picked and processed in an old stone press. Meals include a free breakfast buffet and a light lunch menu. The dinner menu focuses on traditional Tuscan cuisine matched with top-notch regional wines, which can be enjoyed during the meal and afterward out on the shaded terrace.

FINE POINTS

Our Family Loved Most: The peaceful setting of its large swimming pool surrounded by beautiful formal Italian gardens.
Rooms: 18 rooms.
Food: Wine cellar with tastings led by a professional sommelier; café/coffee shop; free breakfast buffet; light lunch; a la carte menu at dinner; children's dinner menu; restaurant serves traditional regional dishes that change seasonally.
Suggested Age for Kids: All ages.
Special Features: In-room Sky television; seasonal outdoor swimming pool; reading area in lobby with fireplace; Wi-Fi and computer rental; meeting space and banquet facilities; wedding services; historic walking trails; mountain bike trails and rental from front desk; customized cooking classes; personal and group wine-tastings; olive mill tours; golfing at Perugia Gold Club 25 minutes from villa—front desk can arrange tee times, transport, and equipment rental; guided excursions to towns throughout the region; Rome and Florence approximately 90 minutes away by train (station is 10 minutes from villa); transport to and from airport.

VILLA GAMBERAIA

Via del Rossellino, 72 | 50135 Settignano – Florence, Italy
Tel. +39 055697205 or +39 055697090 | Fax: +39 055697090
E-mail: villagam@tin.it | Web site: www.villagamberaia.com

Exclusive Luxury Family Offer: Complimentary fruit basket and flowers upon arrival; free access to Villa Gamberaia's famous Renaissance-era gardens and breakfast included in the price on the first morning of stay, arranged upon arrival. Please reference at time of reservation: LFHR-09.

VILLA GAMBERAIA is located on a hillside in Settignano, overlooking Florence and the surrounding Arno valley. The quintessential Tuscan villa, it was completed in the early 17th century by the Florentine noble Zanobi Lapi and combines features of both an urban palazzo and suburban villa. Famous for its Renaissance-era gardens, which are celebrated throughout the world by leading landscape architects and garden historians, Villa Gamberaia is a tranquil spot that rewards inquisitive visitors with a wealth of beauty and charm. Perfect for families, guest accommodations include four fully furnished apartments that sleep six to eight and nine double rooms in the main villa. Here, there is also a large living room leading to a furnished terrace and garden, a dining room, large kitchen, laundry, and an elevator. Two elegantly appointed salons, interior colonnaded courtyard, and various meeting spaces are available for receptions, conferences, exhibitions, and other functions. All of the guest areas reflect the overall architectural theme of cozy Tuscan elegance, mixing family antiques with the modern conveniences and appliances required by today's traveler. Outdoors, you are everywhere surrounded by blooming flowers, sculptured topiaries, lemon groves, and incredible views of Florence, which itself is only a short ride away by car. The pool at Villa Gamberaia is private and secluded, lending itself to a true escape. It's a wonderful spot by which to prepare light meals, eat, and enjoy a bottle of wine. There is no on-site restaurant, but the nearby village of Settignano is filled with grocery shops, *pizzerias*, *enotecas* (wine bars), a *gelateria*, and cafés serving local specialties. This is a great place to stop on your way to or from Florence, and the scenic ride showcases a part of the region into which most travelers rarely venture.

FINE POINTS

Our Family Loved Most: The feeling of living exactly as a Florentine noble would have lived over 400 years ago, surrounded by the breathtaking beauty and symmetry of nature.
Rooms: 4 apartments that sleep 6–8; 9 double rooms.
Food: On-site kitchens for self-catering; variety of options in nearby Settignano.
Suggested Ages for Kids: All ages.
Special Features: Stocked kitchens; housekeeping; Renaissance-style gardens famous for having retained their character virtually untouched for over 400 years; nymphaeum, fountains, and lemon garden; meeting and banquet rooms; swimming pool; children's activities; free parking.

VILLA LA MASSA

Via della Massa 24, 50012 Candeli | Florence, Italy
Tel. +39 05562611 | Fax: +39 055633102
E-Mail: info@villalamassa.it | Web site www.villalamassa.it

Exclusive Luxury Family Offer: 10 percent discount on rack rates during May, June, September, October, and November; 20 percent discount on rack rates during July and August; Offer subject to hotel availability. Please reference at time of reservation: LFHR-09.

VILLA LA MASSA is a 16th-century Medici palace elegantly perched on the banks of the Arno River south of Florence. It received new life as a hotel in 1950, with a careful restoration that retains its aristocratic Renaissance splendor. With its twenty-two-acre park-like surroundings, lush gardens, and lavish décor, the villa is certainly perfect for a private, romantic holiday. But don't let the opulence fool you—Villa La Massa caters to families as well. Younger guests are given the star treatment with gifts upon arrival, milk and cookies before bedtime, mini-bathrobes, and special toiletries. There are a host of activities designed to engage their interests both indoors and out, and when Mom and Dad want to spend some time alone, qualified babysitters are available with a twelve-hour notice. Although the hotel provides daily complementary shuttle service to Ponte Vecchio in the heart of Florence, staying put has its own rewards. There is a heated swimming pool surrounded by gardens and lounges for sunbathing. The fitness and wellness center features the latest exercise machines and a range of massages: deep tissue, relaxation, lympho drainage, aromatherapy, and reflexology. Nearby is a riding school, a tennis club with sixteen red clay courts, and jogging paths lined with fragrant olive trees along the Arno. The hotel provides mountain bikes, and the knowledgeable staff can advise on the most interesting routes into the countryside. Dining at Villa La Massa is under the direction of executive chef Andrea Quagliarella, who uses organic products and produce of the highest quality. Menus include both Tuscan and Mediterranean specialties accompanied by a wine list representing 250 of the best Italian wines with emphasis on Tuscan vintages.

FINE POINTS

Our Family Loved Most: Sitting in the Villa's outdoor restaurant along the Arno, watching the sun play against its surface.
Rooms: 35 rooms. The entire hotel may be rented for private use.
Suggested Age for Kids: All ages.
Food: Medicean Bar & Pool Bar; Il Verrocchio restaurant serving breakfast, lunch, and dinner; wine cellar featuring wine and cheese pairings for private parties.
Special Features: Conference and banquet facilities for meetings, weddings, and other special events; Internet access and computer usage; fitness and treatment room; babysitting service; outdoor swimming pool; variety of sporting activities nearby including riding, tennis, jogging, and golf; amenities for kids include small robes and slippers, crayons and drawing book, chocolate chip cookies and milk at turndown, kids area in hotel park, and board games and other games in the library; complimentary daily shuttle to and from Florence; wine and food activities.

VILLA MARSILI

Viale C.Battisti, 13 - 52044 Cortona (AR), Italy
Tel. +39 0575605252 | Fax: +39 0575605618
E-mail: info@villamarsili.net | Web site: www.villamarsili.net | www.arbitarelastoria.it

Exclusive Luxury Family Offer: SPECIAL TUSCAN WINERY VISIT & TASTING: Book a 2 night stay at Villa Marsili, enjoy a wine tasting in a very well-known winery. This service requires an advance reservation. Please note, the wine tasting can be made from Monday through Friday; not available weekends or holidays. Please reference at time of reservation: LFHR-09.

VILLA MARSILI is one of our favorite hotels in Cortona, which is located on a hillside six hundred meters above the Valdichiana. The quintessential Tuscan hill town, Cortona is where American author Frances Mayes penned her famous memoir, *Under the Tuscan Sun*. Today, more people than ever trek to this sun-dappled city, which is equally renowned for the warmth of its people. That warmth is perfectly reflected in Villa Marsili, where manager Stefano Meacci and his support staff take special pride in making every visit a homecoming. Originally a 14th-century church that was converted into a palazzo in the mid-1700s, Villa Marsili has been renovated into an inviting hotel, whose twenty-seven rooms and suites are all beautifully decorated with plush furnishings, fine antiques, and frescoed ceilings. Many also offer spectacular views of the Valdichiana, the Amiata and Cetona mountains, and Trasimeno Lake. Nearly three thousand years old, Cortona reflects the influences of Paleolithic, Etruscan, Roman, Medieval, Renaissance, and modern cultures. As a result, guests to the hotel are within walking distance to the myriad sites, museums, art, and architecture representative of Cortona's rich culture and history. Evenings encourage lively discussion of the day's explorations, often accompanied by an aperitif or espresso by the cozy fire in the hotel's sitting room or outdoors on the patio or in the gardens. Come morning, refuel with a bountiful breakfast spread, one of the best we've ever enjoyed at an Italian boutique hotel. While there is no on-site restaurant for lunch or dinner, Cortona boasts many wonderful eateries. Our favorite is La Bucaccia, an experience in authentic Tuscan cuisine you'll remember long after returning home.

FINE POINTS

Our Family Loved Most: The hotel's centralized location and the warmth and generosity of management and staff.
Rooms: 27 rooms, including 6 deluxe and 3 suites.
Food: Breakfast; easy access to many fine eateries, including La Bucaccia.
Suggested Ages for Kids: 8 and up.
Special Features: All rooms feature individual climate control, safe, mini-bar, satellite television, and Internet access; Jacuzzi bathtubs in the 3 suites and 6 deluxe rooms; 24-hour concierge; bookings for sightseeing and shopping excursions, cooking classes, and wine tastings; free parking nearby; laundry service Monday through Friday with 24-hour turnaround; car rentals and transfers; babysitting upon arrangement; horseback riding, golf, tennis, and swimming all nearby.

RISTORANTE LA BUCACCIA

Via Ghibellina, 17 | Cortona (AR)
Tel. & Fax: +39 0575606039
E-mail: tipici@labucaccia.it | Web site: www.labucaccia.it

> Within minutes of stepping into Ristorante La Bucaccia, you are no longer a stranger. Instead, you are showered with the kind of hospitality that makes you feel less like a customer and more like a member of the family.

Located in the restored wine cellar of a 13th-century palazzo in the heart of medieval Cortona, Ristorante La Bucaccia is owned and operated by Romano Magi and his wife, Agostina, with assistance from their charming and knowledgeable daughter, Franceschina. Together, the Magi family creates a dining experience that is the perfect expression of Tuscan culinary traditions from the Arezzo region: simple, refined, and harmonious in proportion and taste. Since opening the restaurant in 1997, Romano has brought nothing less than the finest local cheeses, meats, olive oils, and produce into his wife's kitchen. As chef, Agostina has earned accolades for her simple yet exquisitely flavored dishes, true to the time-honored Tuscan ability to "make a lot out of little." In her hands, dishes like chestnut ravioli or noodles with garlic sauce become masterpieces of color, texture, and flavor. She works a similar magic with the meats of the Valdichiana: Cortonese beefsteak, roast cured pork, and wild boar. All are served with their traditional accompaniment of Tuscan white beans in an earthenware pot. Try to save room for Agostina's handmade desserts, which include everything from fruit pastries to tiramisu. The restaurant's wine cellar, the Vineria Cacioteca, offers over two hundred different regional wines, a quarter of which are from vineyards along the Arezzo wine route. In addition to lunch and dinner, La Bucaccia also features a cheese-tasting course and cooking classes, which are designed to further introduce guests to the products and methods traditional to Cortona and Tuscan gastronomy.

VILLA MILANI

Loc. Colle Attivoli, 4 | 06049 Spoleto, Italy
Tel. +39 0743225056 | Fax: +39 074349824
E-mail: info@villamilani.com | Web site: www.villamilani.com

Exclusive Luxury Family Offer: Stay 4 nights and pay for 3, in either a superior double room from €320 or deluxe double room from €380 per night. Breakfast, services, and taxes included. Complimentary bottle of Prosecco sparkling wine in room upon arrival. Extra bed for one child included free of charge. Valid year round, upon availability. Please reference at time of reservation: LFHR-09.

VILLA MILANI is situated a few kilometers from the historical centre of Spoleto, in a splendid position perched right over town. Surrounded by acres of natural meadows and woods, the villa has been ably restored by owners Luigi Capobianchi and Giovanna Milani, granddaughter of the home's original architect, into a first-rate hotel. Built in 1880 by architect Giovanni Battista Milani as his personal country residence, it expresses his devotion to the Classical and Renaissance characteristics of Roman architecture. Milani's refined taste is epitomized in the hotel's salon, with its marvelous ceiling, fine gold decorations, monumental fireplace, magnificent portal, antique furniture and art, and impressive library of 18th- and 19th-century architectural books. Even more refined is management and staff's dedicated Italian hospitality. Each of the rooms, all named after constellations, are beautifully designed for comfort and convenience. One of them, located in the tower, offers wraparound views of the valley below. Guests are encouraged to wander the property to their heart's content—through the lovely gardens, along the statue-dotted terrace with its panoramic views of Spoleto and the Assisi valley, and the beautifully landscaped infinity pool that also offers circular hydromassage. Make sure as well to tour Spoleto, home to the famed Festival dei Due Mondi (festival of two worlds) and other delights. Villa Milani's bucolic setting is the perfect locale for family gatherings, and the terrace and the gardens are popular spots for weddings, parties, and other celebrations. Meals highlight Umbrian specialties crafted from vegetables and herbs from the kitchen garden, extra-virgin olive oil from the property's olive tree groves, and fresh truffles, mushrooms, and wild asparagus from surrounding region—all accompanied by the finest wines from the hotel's extensive cellars.

FINE POINTS

Our Family Loved Most: The awe-inspiring panoramic view of the Assisi valley and Spoleto from the swimming pool, dining terrace, and our guestroom.
Rooms: 11 rooms.
Food: Daily bar service featuring a wide range of soft drinks, beer and wine, cocktails, spirits, snacks, and canapés; breakfast, lunch, and dinner served April through October.
Suggested Ages for Kids: All ages.
Special Features: Room service; business services; fax machine; swimming pool; gardens; terrace with splendid views of the valley and ancient Roman ruins; hydromassage; tennis, golf, horseback riding, gym and sauna, and jogging all nearby; laundry service; cribs available for families traveling with infants; non-smoking rooms; tours of nearby sights.

TRATTORIA LA PALOMBA

Via Cipriano Manente 16 | 05018 Orvieto, Italy
Tel. +39 0763343395 | Fax: +39 0763343395

> Trattoria La Palomba is the kind of restaurant that inspires lifelong loyalty from the locals and passionate *oohs* and *aahs* from visitors. Even the most stringent food critics are known to wax rhapsodic.

John Henderson of *The Denver Post*, who is known for his pithy—and sometimes scathing—year-end roundups of all things culinary, named Trattoria La Palomba's homemade pasta with wild boar sauce as Best Italian Meal for 2007. Our family agrees. In fact, we often drive over an hour from Rome to eat at this wonderful restaurant, located in the heart of Orvieto next door to the 13th-century Palazzo Comunale. For five decades, this family-owned and -operated restaurant has delighted diners with typical Italian warmth at the front of the house and exceptional culinary expertise back in the kitchen. Chef Giovanna uses nothing less than prime seasonal produce, meats, and locally crafted accompaniments to create the best in traditional Umbrian dishes. Starters include *bruschetta* with extra-virgin olive oil and freshly grated truffles, our family's favorite. Oh, those truffles—so earthy and divine! Choose from several wonderful pasta courses like the *tagliatelle* with chicken or *penne* Arrabbiata. Local delicacies like pigeon, tripe, and lamb finish off the main part of the meal. Save room for dessert, too. They're all made fresh on the premises and include wild berry pie, hand-churned ice cream, and the Umbrian classic, *tozzetti* (almond cookies) with Vin Santo. Speaking of wine, the restaurant's impressive list highlights the best local, regional, and national vintages. Your servers will be delighted to discuss the merits of each particular wine in relation to your meal of choice.

VILLA OLMI RESORT

Via degli Olmi 4/8 | 50012 Bagno a Ripoli | Florence, Italy
Tel. +39 055637710 | Fax +39 05563771600
E-mail: info@villaolmiresort.com | Web site: www.villaolmiresort.com

Exclusive Luxury Family Offer: A 5- OR 7-NIGHT MINIMUM STAY IN THE LA COLONICA APARTMENTS INCLUDES: complimentary buffet breakfast served in the restaurant or out on veranda. A 5-night minimum stay includes 1 night free of charge, from €4.000 during low-season period; from €5.600 during high-season period. A 7-night minimum stay also includes wine-tasting in Private Cave and 2 nights free of charge, from €5.000 during low-season period; from €7.000 during high-season period. Upon request, cooking class with chef in La Colonica kitchen. Prices in the Colonica: from €1.000 per night in the low season; from €1.400 per night in the high season. Please reference at time of reservation: LFHR-09.

VILLA OLMI RESORT is located amid the splendid greenery of a fifteen-acre, centuries-old park in the hills of Bagno a Ripoli, just outside Florence. Owned by a series of patrician families from the 1400s to the 1900s, the villa has been restored to its former splendor thanks to several trade guilds working in cooperation with the Superintendent of Florentine Monuments. Transformed into one of Florence's most exceptional five-star properties, Villa Olmi offers guests the utmost in proficient service, privacy, luxury accommodations, and peaceful outdoor settings. Rooms and suites are available at one of three residences, each of which imparts the classical elegance of a Florentine country home—wood and terra cotta ceilings, limestone plaster or frescoed walls, and *Impruneta* terra cotta floors. La Colonica, the former farmhouse, is especially perfect for family and group stays, with two, four-bedroom apartments and an open kitchen. Augmenting the architecture are beautiful antiques and furnishings from Antichita Miccio, Florence's premier antiquarian gallery. Located only minutes from the heart of Florence and from the surrounding Chianti and Valdarno areas, trips into the city or the countryside are readily made by car, train, or the hotel's guided shuttle. Be sure to soak in the splendor of the resort itself, whether by the beautifully landscaped pool or in the colorful park and gardens. Afternoons are perfect for tasting one of the wine bar's 250 vintages while sharing travel stories with other guests. The hotel's gourmet restaurant, Il Cavaliere, is presided over by a young Italian chef known for his eclectic international and Tuscan-based cuisine. He is also exceptionally personable, taking care to check in with guests to ensure their dining experience is nothing less than superlative.

FINE POINTS

Our Family Loved Most: The fascinating journey into the heart of Tuscan cuisine by the hotel's energetic, highly original chef, joined by extraordinary wine pairing of the sommelier.
Rooms: 40 rooms, 10 suites.
Food: Wine bar; breakfast buffet; lunch and dinner at Il Cavaliere restaurant.
Suggested Age for Kids: All ages.
Special features: 24-hour reception; room service; swimming pool; small gym; library; TV room; meeting rooms to accommodate up to 100 people; wine cellar; Wi-Fi inside and out; complimentary toiletry line; daily newspapers; laundry service; cooking classes; personalized guided tours; personal shopper; babysitter; in-room wellness treatments; guided free shuttle service to and from the center of Florence; transfers to and from the airport and rail station upon request.

The cities shown in red represent locations of Luxury Family Hotels & Resorts.

160 | ITALY LUXURY

Southern Italy

A land whose beauty encompasses everything from rugged mountains and craggy coastlines to white-sand beaches and stunning turquoise seas, Southern Italy attracts visitors who seek not only a luxury travel experience, but one that affords privacy as well. You can happily wander through dozens of historic towns and charming villages devoid of the usual throngs of tourists, or tuck yourself away in a chic Sardinian island resort. In fact, this island paradise, along with Sicily, perfectly balances hidden getaways with elite hot spots; it is only a matter of how much you wish to see or be seen. Whatever your choice, you can also count on the fact that your travels will be augmented by a local hospitality as warm and inviting as the ever present sun, all accompanied by plenty of the region's famously tempting food and drink.

Molise

This region is located in south-central Italy, between the Apennines and the Adriatic coast. Molise is known for its beautiful, natural wilderness and time-honored lifestyle. Its rolling hills are strewn with castles that overlook medieval villages and ancient ruins. It is divided into two provinces: Campobasso and Isernia. Campobasso, the capital, is well known for its procession of the "Mysteries," occurring during Holy Week and marked by a somber procession and passion plays. The streets of the town are full of activity, with masses of people who come from throughout Italy for the occasion. The Mysteries are living pictures enacted by men, women, and children, symbolically representing the major feasts of the Church and episodes from the Bible. The town of Isernia rises in the western part of Molise, and it dates back as far as the prehistoric era when the community of the first Europeans resided in one of its valleys. Isernia and its surrounding locales remain unscathed by

The suites of San Domenico Palace Hotel, located atop the chic town of Taormina, Sicily, epitomize a luxurious experience.

FAMILY HOTELS & RESORTS | 161

OPPOSITE: The Grand Hotel Excelsior Vittoria occupies a breathtaking location just off Sorrento's main square on a seaside cliff overlooking the Bay of Naples and Mount Vesuvius. THIS PAGE: Hotel La Coluccia's restaurant offers an excellent choice of Sardinian and international specialties presented with an impressive choice of wines.

tourism, preserving the anonymity and charm of an unrevealed Italy. Located in Isernia is the Museum of Santa Maria delle Monache, which includes two sections, one dedicated to the Paleolithic period and another to remains from the Samnite period. The town also contains the Sanctuary of St. Cosma and St. Damian, the Fraterna Fountain, St. Peter's Cathedral, and the adjacent entrance hall that comprises a part of the podium of a temple dating back to the Roman Republic. Each year in June, the donkey race takes place in the Venafro amphitheater, where contestants ride bareback donkeys and race in a circle. The craft shops of Isernia still create and sell their age-old flutes, bagpipes, and tambourines.

Classic Cuisine: The Molisani were shepherds who journeyed with their herds to Puglia. Because they traveled often, their dishes reflect effortlessness in preparation and time. Consequently, vegetables and cheeses, along with pasta, grains, and fruits, are the key ingredients of their diets. The seasonings of Molise are primarily *il diavolillo* (hot chili peppers, garlic, olive oil, and tomatoes) as prepared in *spaghetti con aglio* and *olio e peperoncino*, which is a spaghetti with garlic, olive oil, and chili peppers. Unique to Molise are a white polenta, *P'lenta d'iragn,* prepared with potatoes and wheat and served with tomato sauce, and *Calconi di ricotta rustica, ravioli* stuffed with Ricotta and Provolone cheeses along with *prosciutto*, then fried in oil. The cheeses of Molise consist primarily of Manteca, Burrino, and Scamorza, or Scamorza *affumicate* (smoked version).

Divine Wine: Formerly, Molise was a part of the Abruzzo wine-producing zone, separated in 1963. Throughout the entire region, there is just one producer of note, Di Majo Norante. The wines are of good character and very individualistic, but quality is variable.

Campania

Renowned as the birthplace of pizza, spaghetti, and *Mozzarella di Bufalo* (Buffalo Mozzarella), Campania is also the region immediately below Lazio, and denotes the true beginning of southern Italy. It has always been a preferred destination, first by the Romans, who coined it the *campania felix* (fortunate countryside). Here, they established themselves in villas and palatial estates that stretched around the bay. The historical significance and renowned beauty of the Campania region is enthralling. Naples, the capital of this province, has numerous sites of cultural and artistic importance. It is home to an aquarium, zoo, Museum of Capodimonte, and the National Archaeological Museum, which houses the important

THIS PAGE: More than a hotel, Cala Caterina is an oasis of tranquility, elegance, and seclusion—a place where the natural and the manmade are seamlessly interwoven to engender total relaxation and rejuvenation. OPPOSITE: At Forte Village Resort, you can choose from a limitless array of restaurants, many of which are a stone's throw from the beach and swimming pool.

finds of Pompeii and Herculaneum. Some of Italy's most renowned sites are located in this region: Mount Vesuvius, the ancient ruinous civilizations of Pompeii and Paestum, the stunning coast of Amalfi, and Sorrento's enchanting peninsula, full of fashionable boutiques, restaurants, and cafés. Days may be spent beach hopping, visiting the chic towns of Positano and Praiano, or taking road trips to the costal summits of Ravello to admire breathtaking views and the magnificent gardens of Villa Cimbrone and Villa Rufolo, the latter having been the inspiration for Wagner's *Parsifal*. Of course, there are also the lovely islands of Capri, Ischia, and Procida, easily accessible for a one-day excursion or a weeklong sojourn.

Classic Cuisine: The volcanic soils of Campania grow some of the best produce in Italy, including San Marzano tomatoes, peppers, peaches, grapes, apricots, figs, oranges, and lemons. Its most famous cheeses are *Mozzarella di Bufalo*, as well as sheep's milk Pecorino, Scamorza, Mascarpone, and Ricotta. Although not native to the region, *Parmigiano Reggiano* is often incorporated into many of the most famous recipes. Moreover, Italian food would not be the same without Campania's spaghetti topped with *pommarola*, their famous tomato sauce; *pizza margherita* (Mozzarella, tomatoes, and basil); *calzone* (stuffed pizza); *caprese* (Mozzarella and fresh sliced tomatoes with olive oil, basil, and ground pepper); and of course *parmigiana di melanzane* (eggplant Parmesan), just to highlight a few of their culinary contributions. The food reveals distinct influences by the various civilizations that have visited these shores throughout the centuries, particularly the French, Greek, Moorish, and Spanish. Along the coastline, seafood is prevalent with *fritto misto di mare,* a mixture of fish fried in olive oil, while other recipes use octopus, cuttlefish, squid, clams, or mussels and prepare them in their own distinct ways. One example is *spaghetti con le vongole in salsa bianca* (spaghetti with clams in white sauce) or *cozze in culla*, which are tomatoes that have been cut in half, the pulp scraped out and filled with capers, parsley, oregano, and bread crumbs. Save room at the end of your meal for *zuppa inglese alla napoletana,* made with Ricotta, chocolate, rum and Liqueur Galliano, Strega, or Amaretto.

Divine Wine: One of the oldest wines produced in Italy is from this region. Known as Falerno today, it is extensively examined to ensure that it matches the original Falernum as closely as possible while achieving modern standards. White Falerno del Massico comes from the local varietal of Falanghina, and is distinguished by floral notes, elegant and pervasive fruit, depth, and good length. Three other good selections from the zone include Taurasi (from the Aglianico grape), Greco di Tufo (Greco), and Fiano di Avellino (Fiano). Taurasi is aggressive and tannic and very long-lived. Greco is crisp and fruity, especially when young, but often improves with a few years of age. Fiano can show considerable grace, refinement, and complexity.

Puglia

Also known as Apuglia, this region comprises the "heel" of the Italian boot, while the Gargano Peninsula is its "spur." Most travelers who venture this far south are taking a boat from Brindisi to Greece; however, this is a region full of enjoyable beaches and charming coastal towns. Its relatively flat terrain makes it an ideal region for biking. Bari is the capital and has preserved its ancient maritime traditions through the centuries. Polignano a Mare is a small and fascinating medieval town in the province of Bari on the Adriatic coast. Polignano presents spectacular caves formed as a result of the constant wave motion of the sea that shaped the calcareous rock. Some of the caves are so deep that they extend downward to the center of the town. The most interesting caves to visit are the Grotta Palazzese, Grotta Stalattitica, and the Grotta della Foca. Some signs of human existence have been found here that date back to the Paleolithic age. Alberobella is a magical land of elf-like, conical white-washed houses made of stones held together without mortar, called *trullis*. According to legend, there are two different versions explaining their construction. Some declare that the Counts of Puglia insisted the dwellings be made in this way, enabling them to be easily torn down should the tax inspectors come to collect money from occupants unable to pay. Others say because the residents only had to pay for permanent houses, the white stones on top of the roof could be easily removed, demonstrating to the inspector that the house was unfinished. Whatever the reason, *trullis* are also immensely efficient — cool in the summer, warm in winter. You can still visit these unique little houses set amid almond and olive trees while watching local

OPPOSITE: Tarthesh Hotel has earned accolades for its restaurant. Its talented chef skillfully augments local and national specialties with fresh herbs and flowers from the property's own gardens. THIS PAGE: Il Melograno Relais & Chateaux is renowned not only for its Mediterranean cuisine and fresh-pressed olive oil from its estate, but also for its superb wines.

residents create ceramics in a method and style that goes back five hundred years. Lecce is an impressive city and is often referred to as the Florence of the Baroque. Just twenty kilometers north of Gargano lay the gem-like Tremiti Islands, a favorite summer weekend retreat for Italians from the neighboring regions. The islands are accessible only by a one-hour boat ride from Termoli, or a three-hour ride from Pascara.

Classic Cuisine: The entire region is a massive farmland that generates copious amounts of tomatoes, grapes, melons, oranges, figs, mandarins, lemons, artichokes, lettuce, wild chicory, fennel, peppers, onions, grains, and olive oil. The locals of Puglia are most proud of their pasta, which very often comprises the heart of the meal. Italy's best durum wheat is used to produce the region's most celebrated pasta, *orecchiette* (little ears), along with other cuts that include *maccheroni, spaghetti,* and *cavatelli*. *Gnocchi* are also popular. A specialty of this area, particularly during Lent, is the *Scalcione di cipolla Puglia,* a calzone with onions, black olives, capers, tomatoes, Pecorino cheese, anchovies, and parsley. The sea brims with fish, particularly cuttlefish, oysters, mussels, octopus, and clams. Try a fresh bowl of *zuppa di pesce*

(fish chowder) or *cozze ripiene,* stuffed mussels with cheese, herbs, and bread. The main meat in Puglia is lamb, served on a spit, roasted, stewed, as well as fried. Sheep's milk cheese is found in abundance, especially fresh Ricotta, Pecorino, and the Mozzarella-like Burrata di Andria. Puglia is also notable for its extraordinary, deep green olive oil. Still, grapes are probably the region's most important crop, produced in vast amounts for both eating and wine-making. A meal in Puglia often concludes with a sweet melon, usually watermelon, and grapes.

Divine Wine: Puglia produces some 17 percent of all wine from Italy, making it a significant and important wine region. Most of this production (30 percent) is from Montepulciano, Sangiovese, and Trebbiano grapes grown in the northern part of the zone. The other notable grape for the region is the Negroamaro ("bitter black"), renowned for long-lived wines with a bitter finish. Negroamaro is mostly blended with the Malvasia grape, and producers like Botromagno are turning out very fine examples.

Basilicata

The Basilicata is surrounded to the north and east by Puglia and the Ionian Sea, to

THIS PAGE: Falconara Charming House & Resort serenely rests on the spot where an ancient castle once stood. OPPOSITE: From your table overlooking the gulf at Villa Las Tronas, you'll be treated to spectacular panoramic views, colorful sunsets, and the finest in Mediterranean cuisine and accompanying wines.

the south by Calabria, and to the west by the Tyrrhenian Sea and Campania. Before the Romans conquered Basilicata, the region was known as Lucania. Although often overlooked by travelers, its captivating, stark mountain scenery has great vacationing possibilities, especially for bona fide travelers with a zest for adventure. Basilicata contains many places of significant interest. At the lakes of Monticchio, walking, biking, boating, and fishing are enjoyable ways to soak in the surrounding natural environment and panoramic views. The large sandy shorelines along the Ionian coast contain many picturesque seaside resorts that resemble those of the Amalfi coast, yet which remain blissfully free of tourism. Maratea, with its attractive surrounding villages, is one of the loveliest resorts along this jagged, rocky coastline of the south Tyrrhenian Sea, and is ideal for boating, diving, fishing, swimming, and snorkeling. The ancient Greek ruins at Metaponto and Policoro, archaeological digs, hilltop medieval towns, churches, and Renaissance frescoes are outstanding. A unique experience, and one not to be missed, is a tour of the "Caves of Matera." These shelters dug out of the tufa rock are considered the first houses of the Neolithic inhabitants of the region.

Classic Cuisine: The woodlands and meadows of Basilicata produce bountiful amounts of fruits, vegetables, legumes, cereals, and herbs with splendid fragrances, especially cumin, chives, rosemary, mint, and wild fennel. The sheep and goats fed on these aromatic herbs produce very savory meats that are then grilled, braised, or baked. Here, pigs are held in high esteem and fed almost exclusively on natural foods, such as beans, corn, and acorns. The result is what many people consider the best pork sausage in all of Italy, the *salsicce lucane* or *lucanica*, a tribute to the region's former name. Another specialty of the region is the *peperone di Senise*, or Senise pepper, traditionally used for flavoring peasant dishes and often used for making local cheeses, cured meats, and for flavoring soups. Cheeses produced in this region are outstanding, and the majority are made from sheep's milk. Pecorino Lucano is of the highest quality and is often used as an ingredient in various culinary preparations. The Cacioricotta cheeses, ancient in their origins, are a timeless blend of goat's and sheep's milk, unifying into a strong and tangy flavor perfect for grating onto pasta dishes. Desserts are also very good, especially those sweetened with local honeys such as *grano dolce* (sweet wheat).

Divine Wine: Basilicata is a one-grape and one-wine region. This grape is the Aglianico. It has produced excellent wines for nearly two thousand years. Believed to be of Greek origin (originally named *Hellenico*), it supports the region's only DOC, Aglianico del Vulture. Producers such as D'Angelo and Paternoster create young wines with vibrant flavor that are full, powerful, darkly fruity, and full of mineral notes. Most are best when consumed within their first ten years.

Calabria

Calabria encompasses the tip of Italy's peninsula, bordered by Basilicata to the north, extending down between the Tyrrhenian and the Ionian seas, and is divided from Italy by the Strait of Messina. The inland area is scattered with small, picturesque villages embracing the hills that slope down to meet the water, along with attractive citrus plantations and olive groves. Calabria has extraordinary landscapes encompassing rugged mountains, infinite wheat fields, and dazzling clear seas. Here is a region with one of the most unrestricted coastline beaches in Europe, making it ideal for boating, swimming, and fishing. Traveling inland towards La Sila Grande, you will come across miles of evergreen forests with snow-capped mountains, streams, and waterfalls. Calabria is home to two national parks: Aspromonte National Park, made up of crystalline granite resembling an enormous pyramid, and Pollino National Park, home to many rare plants

OPPOSITE: Endless beaches and vistas abound throughout Sicily's southern coast. Shown here: Falconara Charming House & Resort. THIS PAGE: Don't even think for a moment that you have eaten cannoli until you've had the famous Sicilian pastry at the San Domenico Palace Hotel.

and animal species and the largest protected area among the recent parks established in Italy. Calabria is one of the regions that has stayed most true to its heritage. In the small villages, elderly men still spend much time playing cards at tables in the town piazzas, as the older woman, still dressed in traditional black, sit together near their homes to chat about the local news.

Classic Cuisine: Most of the cuisine of Calabria is greatly influenced by the Mediterranean. The foods of the region primarily consist of fresh pastas, vegetables cooked in a variety of ways, and meats, though mainly pork. Eggplant is a favorite vegetable and is creatively prepared in a few variations. *Involtini di melanzane con salsa di pomodoro* are eggplant rollups stuffed with Mozzarella and Parmesan cheese, fresh herbs, and breadcrumbs, then topped with a light tomato sauce. Even with an abundance of fish, the region holds pasta in the highest regard, with each city or town specializing in its own dish. Calabrians pride themselves in creating perfect pasta sauces as well, carefully matching each one to create the tastiest dish possible. The varieties are seemingly endless, running from seafood and meat sauces to those that incorporate tomatoes and a variety of other vegetables. Black pepper and *pepperoncini* are extensively used as seasonings, giving Calabrian food its notoriously spicy flavor. Calabrian cooks also pride themselves on utilizing only the freshest seasonal ingredients possible.

Divine Wine: Most of Calabria's wines come from the Cirò zone on the Ionian coast. The red wines coming from the Gaglioppo grape tends to have less color and more tannin than those from Puglia's Negroamaro, but display similar flavors. The white wines from the same zone are typically made from Greco grapes and are normally less distinctive than their red counterparts. The best producers in the region are acknowledged to be Librandi on the Ionian side, and Odoardi of Cosenza on the Tyrrhenian side.

Sicily

Sicily is the largest island in the Mediterranean, and it is considered the most important economically. It is also justly famous for its

THIS PAGE: Chef Massimo Mantarro generates a magical atmosphere of fantasy through his rousing Sicilian gastronomy at Principe Cerami Restaurant at the San Domenico Palace Hotel. OPPOSITE: Sardinia's Sofitel Thalassa Timi Ama's private white sandy beach is just one way in which this five-star hotel exudes savoir-faire. It also features stylish décor, gourmet restaurants, and world-class spa facilities for the ultimate luxury experience.

historical and artistic heritage. The island is encircled by the Tyrrhenian Sea to the north, the Ionian Sea to the east, and the Sicilian Sea to the southwest. The Strait of Messina separates the island from Calabria. Sicily is the most expansive region in Italy. It encompasses the outlying Pelagie Islands, Ustica, Egadi, Pantelleria, and the Aeolian Islands, which consist of Lipari, Salina, Stromboli, Panarea, Vulcano, Alicudi, and Filicudi. On the Aeolian Islands, you will find stunning panoramas, volcanoes, ancient castles, archaeological museums, a variety of water sports, excellent fishing, and fine beaches. Sicily abounds with many wonderful places of interest: Agrigento is a city of exceptional archaeological heritage;

Catania is positioned on the Gulf of Catania and stretches over the southern base slopes of Europe's highest active volcano, Mount Etna; Ragusa is one of the most authentic Sicilian areas, with quintessential towns, magnificent wide sandy beaches, and crystal-clear seas; Syracuse exudes a strong connection with its ancient Greek past, both from a mythological and historical point of view; Palermo is Sicily's largest and most modern city, while Taormina is a captivating medieval town with unrivaled views of Mount Etna and the Ionian coast, along with a truly chic ambience.

Classic Cuisine: The cuisine of Sicily is distinctive from most other Italian regions. The Greeks, Romans, Arabs, Normans, French, and Spanish have all had some bearing on the island's cuisine. There exists an imaginative combination of sweet and sour essences. The generous use of aromatic herbs, exceptional olive oil, abundant fresh seafood, decadent desserts, succulent fruits, olives, almonds, and prickly pears sets Sicilian cooking apart from all others. Sicilians also adore their seafood, prepared in popular dishes such as grilled snapper, *Pesci Spada con Salsa Arancione* (swordfish with orange sauce), and *Tonno con Capperi* (tuna with capers). *Vitello al Marsala* (veal marsala) is the most popular meat dish, but is only one of the countless meat specialties of the region. Pasta is consumed daily in such famous dishes as *cannelloni* (stuffed pasta with meat, cheese, nutmeg, and pepper), or served with a rich, spicy tomato sauce. Some typical Sicilian an-

tipasti are: *caponata*, a pâté-like mixture of eggplant, olives, capers, and celery served on crusty bread, and *arancini*, which are fried rice balls stuffed with beef, chicken, and cheese. Some other characteristic dishes that incorporate the typical produce of the land are *Spaghetti alla Norma*, prepared with fried eggplants, basil, and Ricotta *Salata* cheese, and *sfinciune*, a *focaccia* served with chopped onions, tomatoes, anchovies, and cheese. Sicilian desserts are outstanding: *cannolis* are cylinder-like pastries stuffed with creamed and sweetened Ricotta cheese; *Cassata alla Siciliana* is the most adored Sicilian cake, usually served at Easter and filled with the identical rich Ricotta filling used in *cannolis*; *cubbaita*, a nougat with honey, almonds, and sesame seeds; and, of course, Sicilian *gelato* (ice cream).

Divine Wine: Throughout history, Sicily has provided three vital components of life—grape, grain, and olive. Sicilians have done well with each, especially the grape. The region's winemaking tradition goes back to antiquity and reached its pinnacle of reknown in the 18th century, when English residents created the first Marsala wines. Dismiss the thought of Marsala only as a cooking wine and try some of the dry or *vergine* offerings. The classic Marsala is a light brown color, but Oro, Ambra, and Rubino are light golden, amber, and ruby-red in color, respectively. The basic wines are fortified and often sweetened, while the best go through a *solera* system, similar to that used for sherry. Beyond Marsala, other wines have improved markedly in the past few years, including those based on the native red grape Nero

d'Avola, and the native white grape Inzolia. There is significant production of Cabernet, Merlot, Syrah, and Chardonnay as well, but many producers remain loyal to the traditional varietals. Representative producers include Fazio and Firriato.

Sardinia

Situated in the middle of the western Mediterranean just twelve kilometers from Corsica, Sardinia is the second-largest island in Italy. Modern-day Sardinia has become a beloved holiday site for both affluent Italians and travelers from abroad. If your ideal holiday includes countless beautiful sandy beaches, small islands with turquoise seas, and some of Europe's most spectacular scenery, you cannot beat Sardinia's western coast. Starting up north with Costa Smerelda, and working down to the Gulf of Cagliari in the south, this is where you will find some of the island's best sailing, reef diving, waterskiing, scuba diving, wind surfing, fishing, biking, rock climbing, and archaeological ruins. World-class boutiques, cafés, and restaurants fill resort towns like Porto Rotondo and Porto Cervo. The city of Cagliari, Sardinia's capital, is not only home to several first-class resorts, but is also well worth a visit in and of itself. Established by the Phoenicians in the 7th century B.C., it features monuments, architecture, and archaeological wonders from the various cultures that arrived in port and left their mark. Highlights include the city's old harbor district; the hilltop *Castello* (castle) with its spectacular views; the Basilica di San Saturnino, one of the island's most important Palaeo-Christian monuments; and the Sardinian Archaeological Museum. Located on the northwest coast, Alghero is considered one of the loveliest towns in Sardinia, and has preserved the architecture and language of its Catalonian past. La Maddalena Archipelago has a few beaches and many historical sites, including Garibaldi's final home and resting place on the island of Caprera nearby. In the town of Castelsardo, it is worth visiting the natural sandstone formations of Santa Teresa di Gallura, the ancient towers and fortifications, the Doria Castle, and the 12th-century church of Santa Maria di Tergu. Sardinians are also people of the land, with many still working as shepherds and farmers further inland.

OPPOSITE: South Sardinia has some of the island's best sailing, reef diving, water-skiing, scuba diving, and wind surfing. Sofitel Thalassa Timi Ama caters to adventurous guests by offering access to a plethora of exciting activities. THIS PAGE: Enchanting and secluded, Hotel La Coluccia is the idyllic spot from which to absorb Sardinia's beguiling atmosphere.

Classic Cuisine: Sardinian cuisine mixes the bounty of both land and sea, centering on bread, pasta, wine, cheese, olive oil, and sweets. Sheep, lamb, pig, and fish are commonly roasted, a preparation that best retains the meat's tenderness while cooking it to perfection. Other specialties include artichokes, wild mushrooms, saffron, and, of course, the prized Pecorino Sardo and Fiore Sardo cheeses, which are produced from sheep and goat and served either fresh or aged. Today, these animals still roam the same pristine terrain that they have for centuries, generating the identical mild and delicious flavors of ancient Sardinia. Spicy fish soups called *burrida* (fish boiled with garlic, fish liver, and chopped walnuts) and *cassola de pisci* (fish soup richly seasoned with spicy tomato sauce) along with lobsters, crabs, anchovies, squid, clams, and fresh sardines are all very popular along the Sardinian coast. Alghero especially is famous for lobster, typically prepared by boiling and simply served with olive oil, salt, and a hint of lemon or incorporated into a sauce over pasta. Should you prefer meat, the famous *malloreddus* (saffron-flavored dumplings) with sausage, tomatoes, sheep or goat cheese, and *culingionis* (filled *ravioli* pockets with Ricotta or goat cheese) is a must. Every special feast-day, such as Carnival, Christmas, and Easter, has its own unique desserts. The basic ingredients are typically almonds, oranges, lime peels, cinnamon, vanilla, raisins, walnuts, sugar, and honey. Often Ricotta or freshly grated Pecorino is incorporated.

Divine Wine: For quite a long time, Sardinia's wines have fallen into two categories: light, fresh whites turned out for summer consumption by tourists in beachfront towns, and heavy reds mostly consumed by the island's residents. Since most of Sardinia's history was under Spanish rule, its best known grape is considered to be Cannonau, which is the same as Spain's Garnacha (Grenache). This leads to warm and alcoholic wines. Among the white grapes, Nuragus grows everywhere on the southern part of the island and produces soft, floral, and unspectacular wines. More important but less widely grown is the Vermintino (again of Spanish origin), which tends to produce lightly spicy and creamy wines. There is a strong local demand for sweet and fortified wines, usually using Malvasia and Moscato grapes, but sometimes the native white Nasco as well. Representative producers in Sardinia include Argiolas, Cpichera, Cherchi, and Santadi.

FALCONARA CHARMING HOUSE & RESORT

HOTEL PHILOSOPHY

Localita Falconara | 93011 Butera (CL) | Sicily, Italy
Tel. +39 0934349012 | Fax: +39 0934349135
E-mail: falconara@mobygest.it | Web site: www.hotelphilosophy.net
GPS address: Castello di Falconara

Exclusive Luxury Family Offer: Complimentary fruit basket and *Dolcetti* (local biscuits typical of area) in room upon arrival. Please reference at time of reservation: LFHR-09.

FALCONARA CHARMING HOUSE & RESORT sits on the southern coast of Sicily along the road connecting Agrigento and Ragusa, and offers breathtaking views from atop its promontory. Opened in 2007 as a Hotelphilosphy property, it embodies the mission set forth by this successful Italian hospitality company to offer guests the perfect holiday experience. Developed on the spot where an ancient castle once stood, the resort includes an entirely new building located two hundred meters from the seashore called the Club House as well as a restored section of the original castle called "La Fattoria." Everything from the wood and stone construction materials to the terra cotta and sandstone color palette and Sicilian and African accents were carefully chosen for their quality, elegance, and contribution to a harmonious balance between art and nature. The rooms are chic, with black stone floors, dark wood four-poster beds, and lots of storage for clothes—perfect for an extended stay. Fun in the sun are the operative words here, whether at the beach or at the scenic outdoor swimming pool. The beauty center with spa, massage treatments, Turkish bath, and gym facilities completes the resort experience. Within easy reach is the nearby medieval castle of Falconara, erected in Norman times to repel the invasion of the Moors; the Valle dei Templi of Agrigento; the Villa del Casale in Piazza Armerina, with its splendid mosaics; Caltagirone, with its locally made ceramics; and the pearls of the Sicilian baroque, Ragusa Ibla, Modica, and Scicli. The Falconara's on-site restaurant serves a buffet breakfast and *a la carte* lunch on the terrace or by the pool. Dinner is the perfect time to experience the restaurant's array of authentic Sicilian specialties integrated within a select regional tasting menu of bold and spicy cuisine that focuses on seafood and perfectly matching wines.

FINE POINTS

Our Family Loved Most: Exclusively private setting, chic décor, and serene beach, which results in not only a pleasurable but outright luxurious experience.
Rooms: 36 double rooms, 3 junior suites in the Club House; 14 superior suites, 8 junior suites, 4 deluxe suites in La Fattoria.
Food: Bar and lounge; restaurant serving buffet breakfast, *a la carte* lunch, and a varied regional tasting menu for dinner.
Suggested Age for Kids: All ages.
Special Features: 24-hour front desk; room service; Comfort Zone Space with spa, massage, facial services, Turkish bath, and gym; swimming pool; tennis courts; meeting and banquet facilities; Wi-Fi access in lobby; babysitting and childcare; shops, restaurants, and cafes located at Licata (11 km) and Gela (20 km).

FORTE VILLAGE RESORT

Villa del Parco and Spa | **Hotel Castello** | **Hotel Le Dune** | **Hotel IL Borgo** | **Hotel La Pineta** | **Hotel Le Palme** | **Hotel IL Villaggio**
S.S.195 Km 39.600 | (I-09010) Santa Margherita di Pula | Cagliari - Sardinia, Italy
Switchboard: +39 07092171 | Booking: +39 070921516 | Fax: +39 070921246
E-mail: forte.village@fortevillage.com | Web site: www.fortevillageresort.com

Exclusive Luxury Family Offer: AT THE HOTEL IL BORGO, PER ROOM/BUNGALOW: buffet breakfast; dinner in the exclusive Bellavista Restaurant (beverages excluded); VIP treatment with welcome drink, champagne, and fruit upon arrival; free access to Mini Club (ages 2–12); 1 family bowling tournament/go-kart ride. From €230 per person, per night. Please reference at time of reservation: LFHR-09.

FORTE VILLAGE RESORT is an exclusive, award-winning resort complex located on the southwest coast of Sardinia just forty kilometers away from Cagliari. Winner of "World's Leading Resort" for ten consecutive years and of Tatler's Best Family Spa of 2007, this fifty-five-acre property of pine forest and lush gardens offers seven individual hotels ranging from four- to five-star deluxe. A favorite vacation spot with locals, traveling families, and even members of the international jet set, Forte Village is the epitome of a world-class resort, complete with unspoiled natural surroundings, attentive but unobtrusive service, and state-of-the-art amenities. Whether your idea of luxury is to sail crystal-clear waters with the family, pamper yourself with restorative spa treatments, or enjoy a romantic candlelit dinner for two served by your very own butler, you can experience it here. All guests have access to over a mile of glittering white beaches; a myriad of exciting sports and leisure activities for adults and children; on-site shopping; and bicycle rentals for exploring off-site. Forte Village also features Thaermae del Forte Village, an exclusive spa located at the Villa del Parco that offers a number of restorative massage, bath, and Thalassotherapy treatments, including soaks in one of six seawater pools and an invigorating sea oil wrap. The resort welcomes children with open arms and accommodates their needs with a variety of special touches, including a dedicated children's restaurant, their very own beachside club, and childcare services. In addition to fourteen bars and twenty-one restaurants featuring regional, national, and international cuisine, the resort also houses an exceptional wine cellar with a tasting menu drawn up by international-level chefs matched with exceptional reserve wines.

FINE POINTS

Our Family Loved Most: The unparalleled variety of spa, recreational, and dining opportunities; the delightful wild parrots that fly throughout the property, adding even more color and excitement to this glorious resort.
Rooms: 63 bungalows at Il Borgo; 181 rooms, including superior, suites, luxury roof, and junior suites at Il Castello; 42 luxury bungalows and 13 suites at Le Dune; 140 bungalows at Le Palme; 102 double and triple rooms at La Pineta; 164 bungalows at Il Villaggio; and 25 rooms and 22 bungalows at Villa del Parco.
Food: Wine cellar with tasting menu; 14 bars; 21 restaurants featuring Brazilian, Indian, Japanese, Italian, and regional Sardinian specialties.
Suggested Ages for Kids: All ages.
Special Features: Thaermae del Forte spa with Thalassotherapy, Thalasso massage, and Turkish bath; gym; shopping at Piazza Maria Luigia; 12 floodlit tennis courts; 9-hole putting green; mini soccer, basketball, and volleyball courts; table tennis, ten swimming pools; water-polo tournaments; golf and SCUBA lessons under the guidance of the resort's qualified instructors; horseback riding; waterskiing; windsurfing; sailing; and SCUBA excursions; 18-hole golf a few kilometers away at Molas Golf Club; the Mini Club, a protected oasis a few steps from the beach designed exclusively to entertain children; nursery and babysitting services; state-of-the-art conference facilities, including videoconferencing.

HOTEL CASTELLO AT FORTE VILLAGE RESORT

HOTEL CASTELLO AT FORTE VILLAGE

S.S.195 Km 39.600 | (I-09010) Santa Margherita di Pula | Cagliari - Sardinia, Italy

Switchboard: +39 07092171 | Booking: +39 070921516 | Fax: +39 070921246

E-mail: forte.village@fortevillage.com | Web site: www.fortevillageresort.com

Member of: Preferred Hotels

Exclusive Luxury Family Offer: IN THE EXECUTIVE MARE ROOM: buffet breakfast; dinner in the exclusive Belvedere Restaurant (beverages excluded); VIP treatment with welcome drink, champagne, and fruit on arrival; daily canapés with house wine in the afternoon; selection of herbal teas at evening time; free access to Mini Club (2-12 years old); 1 family bowling tournament /go-kart ride. From €325 per person, per night. Promotion subject to hotel availability. Please reference at time of reservation: LFHR-09.

HOTEL CASTELLO is an exceptional luxury hotel that specializes in creating the pleasure of a holiday in great style. It is one of seven hotels that compose the award-winning fifty-five-acre Forte Village Resort, which is located on the Sardinian coast just outside Cagliari. Hotel Castello takes full advantage of its seaside location and provides its guests with some of the resort's most spectacular views of crystal-clear waters and sparkling beaches, especially from those rooms whose terraces and balconies face seaward. Those that don't face the beach offer instead views of the tranquil parcels of pine forests that dot the property. Located on the fourth floor and overlooking the sea like the ancient watchtowers that used to guide Italy's ships to safety, the hotel's eight luxury suites are designed to showcase boundless vistas of the sea and sky. They are, quite simply, the most exclusive we've yet experienced, each one featuring the luxury décor and amenities expected from a five-star property as well as expansive terraces perfect for enjoying a good book, a romantic meal, or a gathering of friends and family. One features its own lap pool while another has a private Jacuzzi. We highly recommend planning at least one soak at sunset—the interplay of colors over the Mediterranean is simply dazzling. To enjoy the pleasures of the sea firsthand, simply step out the hotel's front door and take a short walk down to the shore. Staying well fed is a cinch as well. The breakfast, lunch, and dinner buffets offered by the on-site Cavalieri restaurant are a true culinary indulgence—the perfect balance between quantity and quality. To complete the experience, talented pianists provide soothing but unobtrusive musical accompaniment throughout the day.

FINE POINTS

Our Family Loved Most: Gorgeous views of the sea from our fourth-floor room. The abundance and variety of the buffets, which easily satisfied everyone's individual tastes.
Rooms: 181 rooms; 8 suites.
Suggested Ages for Kids: All ages.
Food: Cocktail bar; buffet-style Cavalieri restaurant; access to all fourteen restaurants located throughout the property for breakfast, lunch, and dinner.
Special Features: All rooms feature bath and shower, individual air-conditioning and heating, telephone with direct line, satellite TV, video player, mini bar, and safe; some rooms inter-connecting, perfect for traveling families; Thaermae del Forte spa with Thalassotherapy, Shiatsu, massage, and Turkish bath; gym; swimming pools; private beach access; shopping at Piazza Maria Luigia; access to the entire sports and recreational opportunities offered at Forte Village.

VILLA DEL PARCO AT FORTE VILLAGE RESORT

VILLA DEL PARCO & SPA AT FORTE VILLAGE

S.S.195 Km 39.600 | (I-09010) Santa Margherita di Pula | Cagliari – Sardinia, Italy

Switchboard: +39 07092171 | Booking: +39 070921516 | Fax: +39 070921246

E-mail: forte.village@fortevillage.com | Web site: www.fortevillageresort.com

Member of: Leading Small Hotels of the World

Exclusive Luxury Family Offer: AT THE VILLA DEL PARCO PER ROOM/BUNGALOW: buffet breakfast; dinner in the exclusive Belvedere Restaurant (beverages excluded); VIP treatment with welcome drink, champagne, and fruit on arrival; daily canapés with house wine in the afternoon; glass of port/herbal teas at evening time; free access to Miniclub (2-12); 1 family bowling tournament/go-kart ride. From €380 per person, per night. Promotion subject to hotel availability. Please reference at time of reservation: LFHR-09.

VILLA DEL PARCO & SPA is a five-star luxury hotel and spa located in a secluded corner of the Forte Village resort, a fifty-five-acre resort complex situated on the southwest coast of Sardinia just forty kilometers away from Cagliari. Nestled amid lush greenery, colorful gardens, and some of Sardinia's most scenic and pristine beaches, Villa del Parco evokes the feeling of a private island paradise. Each of the hotel's rooms and bungalows feature the beautiful décor and upscale amenities expected of a luxury hotel, while its charming terraces, gardens, and balconies create a decidedly beach house experience. The hotel's four Beachcomber and four Boat House suites offer even greater exclusivity. Nestled among fragrant lemon trees and herb gardens, they feature two swimming pools, private terraces and gardens, private walkways to the beach, and individual butler service. The resort's exclusive Thaermae del Forte, considered one of the best Thalassotherapy spas in the world, is mere steps away. With six seawater pools of varying temperatures plus a series of curative treatments that mix the elements of the sea—water, sand, and seaweed—the spa's treatments are designed not just to pamper the body, but also to detoxify, reenergize, and restore the whole person to optimal health. It is, quite simply, one of the best spas we have encountered. Naturally, after spending the day restoring the body, mind, and spirit, one must spend the evening indulging the senses. To that end, Villa del Parco's exclusive restaurant, Belvedere, fulfills that mission perfectly. Located on the top floor of the hotel, Belvedere offers guests a highly refined culinary experience inside or out on the scenic terrace. All meals are accompanied by a definitive selection of fine wines, exemplary service, and stunning views.

FINE POINTS

Our Family Loved Most: The mix of exclusivity and family friendliness, which made us feel not only special, but also right at home.
Rooms: 25 rooms; 22 bungalows (double and triple); 4 Beachcomber suites; 4 Boat House suites.
Suggested Ages for Kids: All ages.
Food: 24-hour room service; breakfast at Il Patio; dinner at Belvedere; access to all fourteen restaurants located throughout the property for breakfast, lunch, and dinner.
Special Features: All rooms feature bath and shower, individual air-conditioning and heating, telephone with direct line, satellite TV, video player, mini bar, and safe; some rooms and all double bungalows are inter-connecting; Thaermae del Forte spa with Thalassotherapy, Shiatsu, massage, and Turkish bath; gym; two swimming pools; private beach access; shopping at Piazza Maria Luigia; access to the entire sports and recreational opportunities offered at Forte Village.

GRAND HOTEL EXCELSIOR VITTORIA

Piazza Tasso, 34 | 80067 Sorrento | Naples, Italy
Tel. +39 0818777111 | Fax: +39 0818771206
E-mail:exvitt@exvitt.it | Web site: www.excelsiorvittoria.com

Exclusive Luxury Family Offer: FOR A MINIMUM STAY OF 3 NIGHTS IN A DELUXE ROOM: Welcome drink on arrival; 15-minute complimentary massage for 2 people; VIP room setup with chocolates, mineral water, and fresh fruit basket on arrival. Valid upon availability year round. From €550 plus 10 percent VAT tax for 2 persons, per night. Please reference at time of reservation: LFHR-09.

GRAND HOTEL EXCELSIOR VITTORIA occupies a breathtaking location just off Sorrento's main square on a seaside cliff overlooking the Bay of Naples and Mount Vesuvius. When it first opened in 1834, the hotel quickly gained a reputation for both its panoramic views and its exceptional service. Today, it remains one of Italy's finest five-star hotels, thanks to the dedication of its founders and longtime owner/operators, the Fiorentino family. Through the years they have preserved the hotel's unique fin-de-siècle styling and period décor, which combines floral frescoes, original antique furnishings and accessories, and beautiful inlaid pieces by local artisans. Exceptional care has also been taken with the hotel's five acres of grounds and park-like gardens. This decidedly romantic setting is augmented with upscale amenities, first-class service, and an array of elegantly outfitted rooms and suites, each of which feature either a garden or sea view. Soak in the warm rays of the Mediterranean sun at the natural marble and teak pool set amid fragrant orange and lemon groves. Or make an appointment at the hotel's Holistic Center La Serra for a series of revitalizing therapies using natural products and essential oils. The hotel also makes it easy to explore the Amalfi Coast. A private elevator descends from the rooftop to the pier below, where you can hire a motorboat to explore the coastline or travel by jet boat or hydrofoil to Capri, Naples, and Ischia. Sorrento itself is a charming town filled with shops, cafes, and *gelaterie*. Everything from local Campania specialties to international haute cuisine is available at the hotel's three restaurants, where the award-winning chef Vincenzo Galano also oversees an extensive wine list of regional and international vintages.

FINE POINTS

Our Family Loved Most: The desserts and ice creams made fresh by hand each day by the hotel's master pastry chefs.
Rooms: 75 rooms; 23 suites.
Food: Pool bar; Vittoria bar and lounge; 3 restaurants: Vittoria, with magnificent vaulted and frescoed ceilings (the adjoining Vittoria Terrace is home of weekly summer buffet/dances); Bosquet, located on the terrace overlooking the gulf; and Piscina, the poolside restaurant.
Suggested Age for Kids: 8 and older.
Special Features: Outdoor adult swimming pool and children's wading pool; children's playground; Holistic Center La Serra; beauty salon; accommodations and catering for meetings, conventions, and special events of up to 250 people; room service; Internet access; direct-dial phones; cable/satellite TV; turndown service; complimentary bathrobe and slippers; rollaway beds and cribs on request; babysitting; transportation to and from airport for extra charge.

HOTEL CALA CATERINA

HOTEL PHILOSOPHY

Via Lago Maggiore | 32, 09049 Villasimius (CA) | Sardinia, Italy
Tel. +39 070797410 | Fax: +39 070797473
E-mail: calacaterina@mobygest.it | Web site: www.hotelphilosophy.net

Exclusive Luxury Family Offer: Complimentary fruit basket and *Dolcetti* (local biscuits typical of area) in room upon arrival. Please reference at time of reservation: LFHR-09.

HOTEL CALA CATERINA is a gem of a hotel overlooking the crystal-clear waters of Sardinia's southeastern coast just outside Villasimius. More than a hotel, Cala Caterina is an oasis of tranquility, elegance, and seclusion—a place where the natural and the man-made are seamlessly interwoven to engender total relaxation and rejuvenation. With its shady, Mediterranean-style colonnades, sunlit interiors, and delightfully frescoed walls, the hotel suggests the timeless quality of an ancient patrician retreat. The rooms are designed with both beauty and convenience in mind, where delightful touches like painted wooden furniture and marble-topped tables are augmented with all the latest travel amenities. Even the walk to the beach is a sensory experience: gently swaying old pine trees and lush Mediterranean greenery lead to a cove encircled by a series of huge boulders, no doubt worn smooth by centuries of pounding, emerald-colored surf. Here, you can enjoy the day worry free on hotel-supplied sun beds, umbrellas, and beach towels. Or, relax out by the pool, which is surrounded by a lovely garden, terrace, and bar. Cala Caterina is only a few minutes' drive from the town of Villasimius and its well-equipped marina. From there you can board a yacht and sail the turquoise waters of the Tyrrhenian Sea or take a boat excursion complete with refreshments to the nearby islands of Serpentara and Cavoli, both protected marine reserves. The front desk staff will be happy to book these trips. After a day spent exploring or relaxing, let the aromas of freshly grilled seafood, garlic, and tree-fresh olive oil tempt your taste buds. These ingredients and more are used to perfection at the elegant hotel restaurant, whose menu is matched by knowledgeable service and an excellent array of local and international wines.

FINE POINTS

Our Family Loved Most: The experience of being in an all-encompassing resort, whose boutique-style enables the utmost in quality and service.
Rooms: 48 rooms.
Food: Bar and lounge; restaurant serving buffet breakfast, *a la carte* lunch, freshly caught seafood grilled to order, and a varied regional tasting menu for dinner; *a la carte* dinner menu available for extra fee. An exclusively private gazebo with garden and sea view is a must for a romantic dining experience, reserved in advance of stay for additional cost.
Suggested Age for Kids: All ages.
Special Features: 24-hour reception; outdoor swimming pool; private beach; porter service; mountain bike, scooter, and car rental from front desk; Comfort Zone Space with massage and facial services; sporting activities 1 km in nearby Porto Guinco include windsurfing, waterskiing, canoeing, sailing, and boat rental; tennis, diving, and horseback riding 3 km away; nature and archaeological excursions by jeep or boat booked at front desk.

HOTEL LA COLUCCIA

HOTELPHILOSOPHY

Località Conca Verde | 07028 Santa Teresa Gallura (SS) – Sardinia, Italy
Tel. +39 0789758004 | Fax: +39 0789758007
E-mail: lacoluccia@mobygest.it | www.hotelphilosophy.net

Exclusive Luxury Family Offer: Complimentary fruit basket and *Dolcetti* (local biscuits typical of area) in room upon arrival. Please reference at time of reservation: LFHR-09.

HOTEL LA COLUCCIA is one of the jewels of the north coast of Sardinia, situated just opposite the Island of Spargi at the beginning of a picturesque bay bordered by the protected area of the Coluccia Peninsula. Enchanting and secluded, it is the perfect spot from which to absorb the magical atmosphere of the island. Opened in 2003, the hotel is a standout of contemporary design and décor, which incorporates polished cement, soft leathers, rich dark woods, and a façade that mimics the shape of a cresting wave. Complementing its modern design are traditional Mediterranean tile roofs and other local motifs, which anchor the hotel in its spectacular setting. As a boutique hotel, La Coluccia is smart and stylish, but at the same time friendly and exceptionally welcoming to families. With its expansive views of both sea and sky, this is the perfect place to relax, unwind, and savor nature. You can soak up some sun at the sculptured swimming pool, wander among Mediterranean pines and cypresses, stroll along the sandy beach, or visit the beauty center for a massage and Turkish bath. There are also water sports, horseback riding, and golf nearby. Be sure to reserve time to take a boat excursion—with on-board refreshments—to one of the neighboring islands like Corsica, and also visit the shops and cafes of nearby Santa Teresa di Gallura. Dining options abound, including room service, a buffet breakfast, and *a la carte* lunches served poolside or on the terrace overlooking the sea. At dinnertime, the hotel's bar and restaurant offer an excellent choice of local and international specialties presented with an impressive choice of wines.

FINE POINTS

Our Family Loved Most: Luxurious poolside dining with spectacular views of the extensive park drifting down toward the sea.
Rooms: 45 double rooms.
Food: Bar and restaurant serving buffet breakfast, local and international specialties, light lunches, a varied regional tasting menu for dinner with *a la carte* menu available for extra fee; snacks and room service on request; exclusive poolside dining reserved in advance of stay for an additional cost.
Suggested Age for Kids: All ages welcome, but maximum occupancy per twenty-square-meter room is 2 adults and 1 child up to 5 years of age on a *Dormeuse* (small sofa).
Special Features: Swimming pool; Comfort Zone Space with massage, facials, Turkish bath, and gym; meeting and banquet facilities; Internet service; 24-hour reception; laundry service; babysitting and childcare upon request; mountain bikes, scooters, car hire, and excursions arranged from front desk.

HOTEL PELLICANO D'ORO

HOTELPHILOSOPHY

Hotel Pellicano d'Oro | Strada Panoramica Olbia-Golfo Aranci | Km 7 – Loc. Pittulongu | 07026 Olbia (SS) Sardinia, Italy
Tel. +39 078939094 | Fax: +39 0789398149
E-mail: pellicanodoro@mobygest.it | Web site: www.hotelphilosophy.net

Exclusive Luxury Family Offer: Complimentary fruit basket and *Dolcetti* (local biscuits typical of area) in room upon arrival. Please reference at time of reservation: LFHR-09.

HOTEL PELLICANO D'ORO is located outside Olbia on Sardinia's northeast coast, which provides guests not only with panoramic views of this enchanting region, but also the ideal starting point from which to explore the entire Costa Smeralda (Emerald Coast). The hotel is directly in front of Tavolara Island and is surrounded by flower gardens, footpaths, and passageways covered with bougainvilleas in bright purples, pinks, and oranges. Its seventy rooms are located in two buildings, one of which fronts the beach and features simple, casual seaside décor. The other sits poolside, exemplifying a more contemporary ambience. Add to the mix plenty of attentive service and direct access to a sandy beach and crystal-clear water, and you have the perfect recipe for a relaxing holiday. It's no problem if you want to get out and about as well. The highly knowledgeable staff will gladly arrange trips to the nearby Maddalena Archipelago, Cala Gonone, and Cala Luna. They can also book windsurfing, canoeing, tennis, horseback riding, and golf excursions. Those who want to shop until they drop will be thrilled to know that Sardinia is famous for its goldsmiths. Excellent shops and boutiques are located nearby in the chic resort towns of Olbia, Golfo Aranci, and Porto Rotondo. Share your discoveries with family and newly made friends at the hotel's lovely beachside terrace, where you are welcome to spend the afternoon hours with a refreshing drink and light snack. Breakfast is included and is served buffet style every morning, while lunch is available from an *a la carte* menu. Dinner is a truly special event, featuring a regional tasting menu augmented by the finest Sardinian wines from the hotel's cellars.

FINE POINTS

What Our Family Loved Most: Watching the sunset over the ocean while enjoying an authentic Sardinian meal from the restaurant's terrace.
Rooms: 70 rooms.
Food: Snack bar; bar and lounge; restaurant serving buffet breakfast, *a la carte* lunch, and a varied regional tasting menu for dinner.
Suggested Age for Kids: All ages.
Special Features: 24-hour reception; outdoor circular swimming pool; Comfort Zone Space with massage and facial services; conference room for up to 100 people; porter service; piano bar; mountain bike, scooter, and car rental from front desk; supermarket, restaurant, bar, tobacconist; Sporting activities available nearby include wind-surfing and canoeing (2 km), tennis (800 m), horseback riding (12 km), and golf at the Pevero Club (30 km); special excursions arranged at front desk to the world-famous Costa Smeralda, Maddalena Archipelago, Cala Gonone, and Cala Luna.

HOTEL VILLA MELIGUNIS

Via Marte 7 | 98055 Lipari (ME) Isole Eolie, Italy
Tel. +39 0909812426 | Fax: +39 0909880149
E-mail: info@villameligunis.it | Web site: www.villameligunis.it

Exclusive Luxury Family Offer: 5 to 10 percent discount according to availability. Please reference at time of reservation: LFHR-09.

HOTEL VILLA MELIGUNIS is situated in the scenic ancient fishermen's quarter on the island of Lipari, close to Marina Corta's port and town square. Part of the Aeolian archipelago about twenty-four nautical miles off the Sicilian coast, Lipari is the perfect island getaway, featuring pristine beaches, exclusive shops, chic cafés, and lively nightlife. The hotel occupies a restored 17th-century villa and is decorated with bright prints, sleek furniture, and modern artwork. Family owned and run by consummate hostess Manuela Tiraboschi d'Ambra, it is also spectacularly scenic, unfailingly romantic, and exceptionally adept at regaling visitors with personalized service and amenities. Its central location makes it easy to visit Lipari's most popular sights, including the monumental fortress of the "castello," the home of many civilizations going back six thousand years. Numerous archaeological treasures and relics are on display at the local museum. If you are interested in architecture, be sure to check out the various churches near the fortress. No visit would be complete without a trip to one of the island's beautiful beaches. During summertime Villa Meligunis provides shuttle service to the exclusive beach of Canneto, where you can rent chairs and umbrellas. Snorkeling, scuba diving, sailing, fishing, and biking trips can all be arranged from the hotel as well. If you prefer a swimming pool, simply go to the top of the hotel and luxuriate in the beautiful outdoor pool with its stunning views of the sea. This is also the location of the hotel's picturesque lounge bar, which serves typical Aeolian specialties. Just looking at the selections is enough to make your mouth water. Add the finest regional wines, ocean and mountain vistas, and spectacular sunsets and you'll be left dreaming of your next visit—and of perhaps never leaving.

Our Family Loved Most: The awe-inspiring sea view, accompanied by splendid cuisine from the rooftop restaurant.
Rooms: 32 rooms.
Food: Free daily breakfast; room service; rooftop restaurant serving local specialties open April through October.
Suggested Age for Kids: All ages.
Special features: 24-hour reception; lounge and TV room; meeting room and business services; laundry service; Internet; babysitting; transport from and to the harbor on request.

IL MELOGRANO RELAIS & CHATEAUX

Contrada Torricella 345 | I - 70043 Monopoli, Italy
Tel. +390806909030 | Fax: +39080747908
E-mail: melograno@melograno.com | Web site: www.melograno.com

Exclusive Luxury Family Offer: 2 nights in interconnecting classic rooms; breakfast each morning; Pugliese cuisine welcome dinner for four (kids menu available); 4 tickets for the Zoo Safari of Fasano, the third-largest zoo in Italy and the country's only safari zoo. From €1,300, taxes included. Valid all year round except for high season, upon availability. Please reference at time of reservation: LFHR-09.

IL MELOGRANO RELAIS & CHATEAUX is located near Bari in Puglia, right on the Adriatic Coast. It is so named because of the abundance of pomegranate trees that grow in the region, along with prickly pear, lemons, oranges, and centuries-old olive groves. A refurbished 17th-century fortified farmhouse onto which a modern wing has been seamlessly added, Il Melograno not only showcases owner Camillo Guerra's extensive collection of art and antiques, but also his dedication to crafting an exceptional five-star retreat that continually raises the bar on comfort, convenience, and impeccable service. From the gleaming white-stuccoed architecture to the artistically decorated rooms to the spring-fed saltwater swimming pool, the hotel has about it the kind of surreal perfection associated with a Hollywood movie. In fact, when Mel Gibson was scouting locations for his film *The Passion of the Christ*, he housed his entire family here. In a region where the sea informs the rhythms of daily life, the hotel naturally provides plenty of opportunities for adults and kids alike to enjoy the gifts of the Adriatic, whether at the hotel's beautiful pool or at the Le Tamerici Beach Club down the road, just minutes away by a free shuttle. You'll also enjoy getting out and about to explore this uniquely multicultural region, which is a mix of both Italian and Grecian influences. Most notable are the *trullis*, beehive-shaped stone structures that top many of the homes and which were built starting in the 13th century as a way to cool off in summer and warm up in winter. The region's cuisine is likewise celebrated at the hotel's restaurant and cooking school, where Pugliese specialties are exquisitely prepared and elegantly served.

FINE POINTS

Our Family Loved Most: The awe-inspiring sea view, accompanied by splendid cuisine from the rooftop restaurant.
Rooms: 31 rooms; 6 suites.
Food: Bar/lounge; Il Melograno Cooking School and Restaurant.
Suggested Ages for Kids: All ages.
Special Features: Indoor and outdoor swimming pools; two tennis courts; golf; jogging track; 1,000-square-meter-spa featuring Hammam, Fango, and mud bath; sauna; fitness; mountain biking; horseback riding; fishing; sailing; kayaking; free shuttle to private beach (open from mid-June to mid-September) at Le Tamerici Beach Club with Thalassotherapy center; babysitting and child care; free parking; meeting/banquet facilities; laundry/valet services; ferry service to Greece and Albany from Bari.

SAN DOMENICO PALACE HOTEL

Piazza San Domenico, 5 | 98039-Taormina Sicily, Italy
Tel. +39 0942613111 | Fax: +39 0942625506
E-mail: san-domenico@thi.it | Web site: www.sandomenico.thi.it

Exclusive Luxury Family Offer: Complimentary pastries and bottle of regional wine with minimum 3-nights stay. Please reference at time of reservation: LFHR-09.

SAN DOMENICO PALACE HOTEL resides inside a former 15th-century Dominican monastery located in the heart of the charming seaside town of Taormina, home to Italy's premier summer film festival. Taormina's fame as a vacation destination goes back to the Byzantine era, and the people who have sought respite here over just the past one hundred years is a Who's Who of international artists, writers, and political leaders. For many, San Domenico Palace Hotel was their hotel of choice, and they left glowing dedications inside the pages of the hotel's famed Golden Book. Today, Taormina remains the place in Sicily to see and be seen, and San Domenico Palace Hotel continues its long-standing tradition of five-star service. While the friars' soft steps and psalmodies no longer echo through the corridors, the hotel's management and staff retain their own form of devotion—to court an atmosphere of enchantment and refinement while ensuring every guest's stay is a memorable one. The rooms, many with views of the sea, are both spacious and luxuriously appointed, and the suites epitomize luxury. One even comes with its own swimming pool. The hotel also boasts manicured gardens resplendent with blooming flowers; a beautiful outdoor swimming pool; the Beauty Stop wellness center; a full-service fitness area; and the elegant bar and lounge, Oratorio dei Frati. The monastery's former scripta scriptorum is now the Boutique, which sells exclusive fashions, precious ceramics, and delicious Sicilian wines and foodstuffs. Further gastronomic adventures are available at the hotel's four restaurants: Il Giardino dei Limoni, an informal luncheon spot; Les Bougainvillees, an outdoor terrace eatery; Antico Refettorio, which showcases locally grown products; and the gourmet Principe Cerami, proud bearer of a Michelin star, thanks to the culinary artistry of chef Massimo Mantarro.

FINE POINTS

Our Family Loved Most: Opulence in the heart of Taormina.
Rooms: 93 rooms; 15 suites; non-smoking rooms available.
Food: Poolside bar; Oratorio dei Frati bar; Il Giardino dei Limoni, Les Bougainvilles, Antico Refettorio, Principe Cerami restaurants. Children under 8 are welcomed at the Principe Cerami only from 7.30 p.m. to 8.30 p.m., and Les Bougainvillèes accepts them later in the evening with advanced booking. Pushchairs and high chairs are not allowed in both restaurants in the evening. The concierge, upon request, can provide a babysitter.
Suggested Ages for Kids: All ages.
Special Features: Room service; meeting facilities to accommodate events and ceremonies for up to 500 people; high-speed Internet at the Internet Corner; the Beauty Corner with massages and personalized treatments; fitness center; manicured gardens; heated outdoor swimming pool; babysitting upon request; historical tours of the monastery twice a week from May to October; shuttle to and from the airport for a fee.

SANT'ELMO BEACH HOTEL

HOTELPHILOSOPHY

Castiadas – Costa Rei | Località Sant'Elmo | 09040 Castiadas (CA) | Sardinia, Italy
Tel. +39 070995161 | Fax: +39 070995140
E-mail: santelmo@mobygest.it | Web site: www.hotelphilosophy.net

Exclusive Luxury Family Offer: Complimentary fruit basket and *Dolcetti* (local biscuits typical of area) in room upon arrival. Please reference at time of reservation: LFHR-09.

SANT'ELMO BEACH HOTEL is a slice of paradise on the southeastern coast of Sardinia, ideal for both couples and families seeking the ultimate beachside vacation. Located 4 km from Costa Rei and fourteen kilometers from Villasimius, it is distinguished by the highest standards of professionalism and quality services as well as abundant greenery, lovely gardens, and stunning views of the sea from its clifftop location. Built in typical Mediterranean style, the hotel comprises a central main building with the majority of guestrooms housed in smaller terraced buildings. All are equipped with satellite television, air conditioning, direct-dial telephone, mini bar, safe, bathrooms with shower, hair dryer, and bathrobe and slippers. The main building not only houses reception, but also a television room, a boutique, and the swimming pool with its terrace/solarium. An entertainment area and play-park for children with a gazebo are situated near the main building, as is a sports area consisting of two tennis courts, a football pitch, a basketball and volleyball court, and a small gymnasium. A short walk on foot or an even shorter shuttle ride brings guests to white-sand beaches, equipped with umbrellas, sun beds, and towels. Several secluded sandy coves are at the disposal of those guests seeking privacy and quiet. In keeping with its array of services, the hotel features no fewer than four restaurants ranging from buffet style to elegant service: the open air Il Corbezzolo with its Sardinian menu of spit-grilled meats; La Rotonda, offering a Mediterranean menu; the exclusive Il Belvedere Restaurant with its glorious sea views from the raised terrace; and the family-style Sant'Elmo Grill Terrace Restaurant. The pool bar and beach bar are open to serve snacks or light lunches throughout the day.

FINE POINTS

Our Family Loved Most: Proximity to some of the most beautiful, unspoiled beaches on the island; the myriad of activities available to both children and adults.
Rooms: 175 rooms, including: Cottage Classic (2–3 people), Cottage Family (2 adults + 2 children), Connecting Cottage (4–6 people), and Junior Suite (2–4 people).
Food: Pool bar; beach bar; Il Corbezzolo; La Rotonda; Il Belvedere Restaurant; Sant'Elmo Grill Terrace Restaurant.
Suggested Ages for Kids: All ages.
Special Features: Piano bar; evening entertainment with games and Italian cabaret; group classes in canoeing, windsurfing, tennis, swimming, aqua-gym, and aerobics. Tournaments of five-a-side football, bowling, volleyball, basketball, table tennis; children's Mini Club (4–7 years), Dolphin Club (8–11 years), and Young Club (12–17 years), with various age-appropriate entertainment programs; boat, dinghy, sail boat, pedaloe, and canoe rentals; windsurfing, waterskiing, and monoskiing; banana boat, diving, and various boat excursions by arrangement; 18-hole mini-golf; riding school 2 km away.

SOFITEL THALASSA TIMI AMA

Localita Notteri | 09049 Villasimus | Sardinia, Italy
Tel. +39 07079791 | Fax: +39 070797285
E-mail: H3040@accor.com | Web site: www.sofitel.com

Exclusive Luxury Family Offer: Fruit basket and a bottle of Cuvée di Prosecco Ville D'Arfanta wine in room upon arrival. Please reference at time of reservation: LFHR-09.

SOFITEL THALASSA TIMI AMA is part of the international Sofitel Luxury Hotel Group, which specializes in combining the unique flavor of its individual locales with the ultimate in refined service and amenities. Located on Sardinia near the small town of Villasimius fifty kilometers from Cagliari International Airport, Sofitel Thalassa Timi Ama is one of the island's premier spots to relax and rejuvenate. Nestled within a Mediterranean Garrigue that gives way to a private, white sandy beach, this peaceful retreat blends the savoir-faire one expects from a five-star hotel—stylish décor, gourmet restaurants, and world-class spa facilities—with Sardinia's distinctive native charm and warmth. General manager Patrick Recasens and his professional staff excel at cheerfully and expertly meeting the needs of every guest, from families with children to single couples and individuals. This is a spot that engenders total relaxation, whether from your poolside lounge chair overlooking the serene Bay of Timi Ami, while strolling along the quiet beach, or during an hour-long yoga class. The on-site Thalassotherapy Institute indulges spa-goers with the very best in massage, reflexology, body wraps, and marine-based treatments. It also has a fitness center with Hammam, Jacuzzi, sauna, solarium, and spa bath, and a full-service beauty salon. Only two kilometers away, Villasimius remains largely untouched by tourism and is filled with great shops and cafes. Gourmet local, regional, and international cuisine is available at three on-site bars and restaurants: I Ginepri, featuring grilled specialties at lunch and Sardinian favorites at dinner; Il Mediterraneo, featuring an international lunchtime menu; and La Veranda, with its sumptuous breakfast and dinner buffets. Each restaurant reflects head chef Joel Marchetto's signature skill at melding the best in French-style cuisine with the latest fusion dishes from around the world.

FINE POINTS

Our Family Loved Most: Gorgeous white sandy beach with wide array of water sports to suit each of our desires; assuring a great time for all.
Rooms: 275 rooms; 4 suites.
Food: Beach, lobby, pool bar; snack bar; I Ginepri, Il Mediterraneo, La Veranda restaurants.
Suggested Ages for Kids: 4 years and older.
Special Features: All rooms feature smoke alarms and sprinklers, 220/240 V AC, RJ11 and RJ 25 outlets, air-conditioning, mini-bar, color satellite/cable TV, high-speed Internet, showers, and bathtubs in superior rooms; Thalassotherapy Institute with massage, reflexology, Shiatsu, sculptures, wraps, stretching, and Pilates; full-service fitness center and beauty salon; Hammam, spa bath, sauna, Jacuzzi, solarium, and swimming pool; private beach access; shopping at Villasimius; sailing, snorkeling, waterskiing, surfing, and fishing excursions by appointment; 4 well-equipped meeting rooms to serve up to 500 persons; free shuttle service from the hotel to Villasimius; private car transport from the airport to the hotel for extra fee.

TARTHESH HOTEL

Via Parigi 3 | 09036 Guspini (CA) | Sardinia, Italy
Tel. +39 0709729000 | Fax: +39 0709764003
E-mail: info@tartheshotel.com | Web site: www.tartheshotel.com

Exclusive Luxury Family Offer: COMPLIMENTARY ROOM NIGHT: book 4 nights, get the 5th night free. Also enjoy 25 percent reduction on massage. Valid upon availability September through June. Please reference at time of reservation: LFHR-09.

TARTHESH HOTEL is located in southwestern Sardinia just outside Guspini. It is truly a magical spot from which to step off the beaten tourist path to relax, rejuvenate, and explore the natural beauty of the region. The hotel's famously warm atmosphere is evident immediately upon entering, emanating not only from the architecture and décor, but also from the hotel's charming owner, Elisabetta Cavalli, and her exceptionally gracious staff. Like the building's exterior, the interior imparts a distinct North African feel, with earth tones juxtaposed against stark black and white. The hotel's entry hall holds the reception area as well as a comfortable reading room and stylish bar and lounge. The rooms, while simply decorated, are exceptionally spacious, with many offering lovely views of the gardens. The heart of the hotel, though, has to be its spectacular swimming pool. Designed out of basalt and lined with myrtles and palm trees, it is where guests relax, socialize with ease, and where they can experience one of the hotel's luxuriant hydrotherapies. Other wellness treatments like massages and mud wraps are also available. Naturally, you'll want to visit the Costa Verde, the forty-seven kilometers stretch of beautiful beaches, coves, and cliffs along Sardinia's western shore. The exciting forty-five-minute drive meanders through unspoiled mountain terrain before ending at the brilliant blue waters of the Mediterranean. Tarthesh has also earned accolades for its restaurant, which offers breakfast, lunch, and dinner and whose talented chef skillfully augments local and national specialties with fresh herbs and flowers from the hotel's own gardens. Guests are of course encouraged to visit the on-site cellar, which houses the hotel's extensive collection of local and regional wines, cheeses, and salamis.

FINE POINTS

Our Family Loved Most: Relaxing poolside, soaking in the easy-going Sardinian way of life.
Rooms: 40 rooms.
Food: Bar and lounge; Tarthesh Restaurant.
Suggested Ages for Kids: All ages.
Special Features: All rooms feature satellite television, radio, Internet access, safe, mini-bar, and air-conditioning; wellness treatments to include massage, hydrotherapy, and mud wraps; highly knowledgeable and accommodating staff can arrange a variety of excursions to suit both children and adults; *Terme* center 10 km away; beach only 45 minutes by car.

VILLA LAS TRONAS

Lungomare Valencia 1, 07041 | Alghero, Italy
Tel. +39 079981818 | Fax: +39 079981044
E-mail: info@hotelvillalastronas.it | Web site: www.hotelvillalastronas.it

Exclusive Luxury Family Offer: Complimentary bottle of wine upon arrival for all guests. Year round special, REAP WHAT YOU SOW: CULTIVATE YOUR KARMA: Dharmic action brings peace and happiness and enables peace and happiness to be sought. For 1–2 persons, 3 days, 2 nights, from €900 for 1 person, from €1,100 for 2 people. Includes stay in standard double room, complimentary breakfast, 1 ayurvedic massage, 1 shirodhara, and 1 udvartana. Please reference at time of reservation: LFHR-09.

VILLA LAS TRONAS was renowned as the place up until the 1940s where Italian royalty spent their holidays in Sardinia. Still resplendent, with its marble floors, high ceilings, crystal chandeliers, antique furniture, and spectacular views, it is now open to the traveling public. Built on a private promontory jutting out into the Gulf of Alghero, the villa offers some of the most romantic, sophisticated, and private accommodations you will find on the Mediterranean. Only a few paces from the center of Alghero, a town blissfully untouched by tourism, the villa's enclosed park has a controlled access that makes the entire property an island in and of itself. The hotel's piers and terraces are perfect for summer sunbathing or winter sport fishing, or you can relax and rejuvenate in the seawater, open-air swimming pool. You can also treat yourself to a body massage, facial treatment, manicure, and pedicure in the beauty center or use the Technogym cardio-fitness equipment in the fitness area. Each room has its own classic style enriched with antiques. Some feature a terrace and sea view; others have either a sea or a garden view. Because the hotel is surrounded by nearly one thousand square meters of coast on three sides, you are treated to spectacular views of the sea from sunrise to sunset. Not only do the rooms come with a view, so does the dining room. From your table overlooking the gulf, you'll be treated to spectacular panoramic views, colorful sunsets, and the finest in Mediterranean cuisine and accompanying wines. A post-dinner drink or cup of soothing tea in the adjacent bar is the perfect way to cap off a magical evening.

FINE POINTS

Our Family Loved Most: Never-ending sea views from every position of the property, especially the dining room and terrace at dusk.
Rooms: 20 rooms; 2 junior suites; 3 suites.
Food: Restaurant offering breakfast, lunch, and dinner.
Suggested Age for Kids: All ages; children under 3 years old are provided with cot free of charge; under 18 years of age, receive 25 percent discount.
Special Features: Sandy dockyard suitable for mooring small crafts; helipad; billiards room; beauty and fitness center with sun shower, manicures, pedicures, waxing, and massage; outdoor seawater swimming pool; park, piers, and terraces overlooking the sea; 5- to 10-minute walk into Alghero; car and boat rentals; private, guided tours of Sanna Museum at Sassari, the local coastline, and the Anghelu Ruju Necropolis and other archaeological sites; wine cellar and wine-tasting tours; free parking, Gourmet's Pleasure Package available for cooking enthusiasts; small pets welcome; transport to and from airport.

ABITARE LA STORIA

Sede di Presidenza e Segreteria | c/o Villa Dal Pozzo D'Annone | S.S. del Sempione, 5 | 28832 Belgirate (Verbania) Italia
Tel. +39 0322772156 | Fax: +39 0322292678 | Cell: +39 3463055743
E-mail: mailbox@abitarelastoria.it | Web site: www.abitarelastoria.it

> Founded in 1995, Abitare la Storia is an association of independent accommodation facilities that are located in historical dwellings throughout Italy.

Situated both in towns and throughout the countryside, these facilities provide guests with the utmost in reliability and professional hospitality services, while at the same time promoting traditional Italian culture. They are designed to accommodate travelers who appreciate the traces of history and art that past centuries have imprinted upon these places.

As an organization, Abitare la Storia seeks to protect and enhance Italy's cultural and ecological heritage. The establishments that operate as part of Abitare la Storia include hotels, restaurants, historical residences, and congress centers, and are located exclusively in buildings of striking architectural and scenic beauty. Each house offers its guests an experience unique to its particular region. In addition, visitors cannot fail to appreciate the warmth and enthusiasm of owner-managers who express nothing less than the highest devotion to their profession.

Abitare la Storia has also developed a series of itineraries linking its various properties, many of which follow back roads still undiscovered by the majority of tourists. These itineraries are designed to promote Italy's many marvelous artistic, scenic, gastronomic, and oenological (wine-making) treasures, many of which, until now, have not received the due respect and attention they deserve.

An Abitare la Storia property is more than just a place to say. By transforming the traveling experience, they provide visitors the chance to discover and live Italy's fascinating past.

DIRECTORY

Albergo Del Sole Al Pantheon
Piazza della Rotonda
63 - 00186 Rome
Tel. + 39 066780441
Fax: +39 0669940689
info@hotelsolealpantheon.com
www.hotelsolealpantheon.com

Albergo Pietrasanta
Via Garibaldi 35
Pietrasanta 55045
Tel. +39 0584793726
Fax. +39 0584793728
info@albergopietrasanta.com
www.albergopietrasanta.com

Borgo Tre Rose
Via I Palazzi, 5
53040 Montepulciano - Valiano (Si)
Tel. +39 0578724491
Fax: +39 0578724227
info@borgotrerose.it
www.borgotrerose.it

Castello di Magona
Via di Venturina, 27
57021 Campiglia Marittima (Livorno)
Tel. +39 0565851235
Fax: +39 0565855127
relais@castellodimagona.it
www.castellodimagona.it

Castello di Vicarello
Localita Vicarello 1
58044 Poggi del Sasso - Cinigiano (Grosseto)
Tel. +39 0564990718
Fax: +39 0564990718
info@vicarello.it
www.castellodivicarello.com

Castello Gargonza
Localita Gargonza
52048 Monte San Savino
Tel. +39 0575847021
Fax: +39 0575847054
info@gargonza.it
www.gargonza.it

Castello Orsini Hotel
Via Aldo Bigelli snc
00017 Nerola (Rome)
Tel. +39 0774683272
Fax: +39 0774683107
direzione@castelloorsini.it
www.castelloorsini.it

Eremo Delle Grazie
Loc. Monteluco 13 - 06049
Spoleto (PG)
Tel. +39 074349624
Fax: +39 074349650
eremodellegrazie@tin.it
www.eremodellegrazie.it

Falconara Charming House and Resort
Localita Falconara
93011 Butera (CL)
Sicily
Tel. +39 0934349012
Fax +39 0934349135
falconara@mobygest.it
www.hotelphilosophy.net
www.mobygest.it

Forte Village Resort
S.S.195 Km 39.600
(I-09010) Santa Margherita di Pula
Cagliari - Sardinia
Switchboard: +39 07092171
Booking: +39 070921516
Fax: +39 070921246
forte.village@fortevillage.com
www.fortevillageresort.com

Hotel Castello at Forte Village
S.S.195 Km 39.600
(I-09010) Santa Margherita di Pula
Cagliari – Sardinia
Switchboard: +39 07092171
Booking: +39 070921516
Fax: +39 070921246
forte.village@fortevillage.com
www.fortevillageresort.com

Villa del Parco & Spa at Forte Village
S.S.195 Km 39.600
(I-09010) Santa Margherita di Pula
Cagliari – Sardinia
Switchboard: +39 07092171
Booking: +39 070921516
Fax: +39 070921246
forte.village@fortevillage.com
www.fortevillageresort.com

Grand Hotel Excelsior Vittoria
Piazza Tasso, 34
80067 Sorrento (Napoli)
Tel. +39 0818071044
Fax: +39 0818771206
info@exvitt.it
www.excelsiorvittoria.com

Grand Hotel Sitea
Via Carlo Alberto 35
10123 Turin
Tel. + 39 0115170171
Fax: + 39 011548090
sitea@thi.it
www.sitea.thi.it

Grand Hotel Visconti
Viale Isonzo, 14
20135 Milan (Milano)
Tel. +39 0254 0341
Fax: +39 0254069523
info@grandviscontipalace.com
www.grandviscontipalace.com

Hotel Ancora
Corso Italia, 62
32043 Cortina d'Ampezzo (Belluno)
Tel. +39 04363261
Fax: +39 04363265
info@hotelancoracortina.com
www.hotelancoracortina.com

Hotel Bellevue
Rue Grand Paradis, 22
11012 Cogne (Valle d'Aoste)
Tel. +39 016574825
Fax: +39 0165749192
info@hotelbellevue.it
www.hotelbellevue.it

Hotel Cala Caterina
Via Lago Maggiore, 32
09049 Villasimius (CA) - Sardinia
Tel. +39 070797410
Fax +39 070797473
calacaterina@mobygest.it
www.hotelphilosophy.net
www.mobygest.it

Hotel Cenobio Dei Dogi
Via Cuneo, 34
16032 Camogli - Portofino Coast
Tel. +39 01857241
Fax: +39 0185772796
reception@cenobio.it
www.cenobio.it

Hotel Dei Mellini
Via Muzio Clementi 81
00193 Rome
Tel. +39 06324771
Fax: +39 0632477801
info@hotelmellini.com
www.hotelmellini.com

Hotel Eden
Via Ludovisi, 49
00187 Rome (roma)
Tel. +39 06478121
Fax: +39 064821584
1872.concierge@lemeridien.com
www.lemeridien.com/eden

Hotel Elephant
I-39042 Bressanone
Via Rio Bianco 4, South Tyrol
Tel. +39 0472832750
Fax: +39 047283657
info@hotelelephant.com
www.hotelelephant.com

Hotel La Coluccia
Localita Conca Verde
07028 Santa Teresa di Gallura
Sassari - Sardinia
Tel. +39 0789758004
Fax: +39 0789758007
calacaterina@mobygest.it
www.hotelphilosophy.net
www.mobygest.it

Hotel Lord Byron
Via Giuseppe De Notaris, 5
00197 Rome
Tel. +39 063220404
Fax: +39 063220405
info@lordbyronhotel.com
www.lordbyronhotel.com

Hotel Palazzo Bocci
Via Cavour, 17
06038 Spello (PG)
Tel. +39 0742301021
Fax: +39 0742301464
info@palazzobocci.com
www.palazzobocci.com

Hotel Pellicano D`Oro
Strada Panoramica Olbia-Golfo Aranci
km 7 - Loc. Pittulongu
07026 Olbia (SS) - Sardinia
Tel. +39 078939094
Fax: +39 0789398149
pellicanodoro@mobygest.it
www.hotelphilosophy.net
www.mobygest.it

Hotel Portofino Kulm
Viale Bernardo Gaggini, 23
Portofino Vetta - 16030 Ruta di Camogli
Tel. +39 01857361
Fax: +39 0185776622
kulm@portofinokulm.it
www.portofinokulm.it

Hotel Regency
Piazza M. D'Azeglio, 3
50121 Florence
Tel. +39 055245247
Fax: +39 0552346735
info@regency-hotel.com
www.regency-hotel.com

Hotel Villa Aminta
Via Sempione Nord
123 28838 Stresa (Verbania)
Tel. +39 0323933818
Fax: +39 0323933955
villa-aminta@villa-aminta.it
www.villa-aminta.it

Hotel Villa Ca`Sette
Via Cunizza, 4
36061 Bassano del Grappa (Vicenza)
Tel. +39 0424383350
Fax: +39 0424393287
info@ca-sette.it
www.ca-sette.it

Hotel Villa Franceschi
Via Don Minzoni, 28
Mira Porte, (Venice) 30034
Tel. +39 0414266531
Fax: +39 0415608996
info@villafranceschi.com
www.villafranceschi.com

Hotel Villa Margherita
Via Nazionale, 416
30300 Mira Porte (Venice)
Tel. +39 0414265800
Fax: +39 0414265838
info@villa-margherita.com
www.villa-margherita.com

Hotel Villa Meligunis
Via Marte 7
98055 Lipari (ME) Isole Eolie
Tel. +39 0909812426
Fax: +39 0909880149
info@villamelegunis.it
www.villamelegunis.it

IL Borro
52040 San Giustino
Valdarno, Tuscany
Tel. + 39 055977053
Fax: +39 055977055
ilborro@ilborro.it
www.ilborro.com

IL Melograno Relais and Chateaux
contrada Torricella 345
I - 70043 Monopoli
Tel. +39 0806909030
Fax: +39 080747908
melograno@melograno.com
www.melograno.com

Locanda dei Mai Intees
Via Nobile Claudio Riva, 2
21022 Azzate (VA)
Tel. +39 0332457223
Fax: +39 0332459339
maiintees@tin.it
info@mai-intees.com
www.mai-intees.com

Lucignanello Bandini
Localita Lucignano d'Asso
53020 San Giovanni d'Asso - Siena
Tel. +39 0577803068
Fax: +39 0577803082
P. Iva 00169080520
info@borgolucignanello.com
www.borgolucignanello.com
www.abitarelastoria.it

Palazzo Barbarigo Sul Canal Grande
San Polo 2765
Venice
Tel. +39 041740172
Fax: +39 041740920
palazzobarbarigo@mobygest.it
www.hotelphilosophy.net
www.mobygest.it

Palazzo Viviani - Castello Di Montegridolfo
Via Rome, 38
47837 Montegridolfo (RN) Emilia Romagna
Tel. +39 0541855350
Fax: +39 0541855340
montegridolfo@mobygest.it
www.hotelphilosophy.net
www.mobygest.it

Park Hotel Villa Grazioli
Via Umberto Pavoni, 19
00046 Grottaferrata (Rome)
Tel. +39 069454001
Fax: +39 069413506
info@villagrazioli.com
www.villagrazioli.com

Relais Campo Regio
Via della Sapienza 25
53100 Siena (Siena)
Tel. +39 0577222073
Fax: +39 0577237308
relais@camporegio.com
www.camporegio.com

Relais & Chateaux Villa La Vedetta
Viale Michelangiolo, 78
50125 Firenze (Florence)
Tel. +39 055681631
Fax: +39 0556582544
info@villalavedettahotel.com
www.villalavedettahotel.com

Relais La Corte dei Papi
Via La Dogana, 12
52040 Loc. Pergo di Cortona (Arezzo)
Tel. +39 0575614109
Fax: +39 0575614963
Cell: +39 3483264823
info@lacortedeipapi.com
www.lacortedeipapi.com

Residenza del Moro
Via del Moro 15
50123 Florence
Tel. +39 055290884 or 055264269
Fax: +39 0552648494
info@residenzadelmoro.com
www.residenzadelmoro.com

Residenza Torre di San Martino
Castello di Rivalta
29010 Gazzola (Piacenza)
Tel. + 39 0523972002
Fax: +39 0523972030
info@torredisanmartino.it
www.torredisanmartino.it

Royal Hotel Sanremo
80, Corso Imperatrice
18038 - Sanremo - Liguria
Tel. +39 01845391
Fax: +39 0184661445
royal@royalhotelsanremo.com
www.royalhotelsanremo.com

San Clemente Palace Hotel and Resort
Isola di San Clemente 1, San Marco
30124 Venice
Tel. +39 0412445001
Fax: +39 0412445800
sanclemente@thi.it
www.sanclemente.thi.it

San Domenico Palace Hotel
Piazza San Domenico, 5
98039-Taormina
Tel. +39 0942613111
Fax: +39 09426255C6
san-domenico@thi.it
www.sandomenico.thi.it

Sant'Elmo Beach Hotel
CASTIADAS - COSTA REI
Localita Sant'Elmo
09040 Castiadas (CA) - Sardinia
Tel. +39 070995161
Fax: +39 070995140
santelmo@mobygest.it
www.hotelphilosophy.net
www.mobygest.it

Sofitel Thalassa Timi Ama
Localita Notteri Sardinia 09049
VILLASIMIUS
Tel. +39 07079791
Fax: +39 070797285
sofitel.timiama@accor-hotels.it
www.sofitel.com

Tarthesh Hotel
Via Parigi 3
09036 Guspini (CA) Sardinia
Tel.+39 0709729000
Fax: +39 0709764003
info@tartheshotel.com
www.tartheshotel.com

Tombolo Talasso Resort
Via del Corallo 3, - 57024
Marina di Castagneto Carducci (LI)
Tel. +39 056574530
Fax: +39 0565744052
info@tombolotalasso.it
www.grandhoteltombolo.com

Villa Campestri
Via di Campestri 19/22
50039 Vicchio di Mugello (Florence)
Tel. +39 0558490107
Fax: +39 0558490108
villa.campestri@villacampestri.it
www.villacampestri.com

Villa di Piazzano
Localita Piazzano
Cortona 06069
Tel. +39 075826226
Fax: +39 075826336
info@villadipiazzano.com
www.villadipiazzano.com

Villa Gamberaia
Via del Rossellino, 72
50135 Settignano - Florence
Tel. +39 055697205 or 055697090
Fax: +39 055697090
villagam@tin.it
www.villagamberaia.com

FAMILY HOTELS & RESORTS

Villa La Massa
Via della Massa, 24
50012 Candeli (Florence)
Tel. +39 055562611
Fax: +39 055633102
info@villalamassa.com
www.villalamassa.com

Villa Las Tronas
Lungomare Valencia 1
07041 Alghero (Alghero)
Tel. +39 079981818
Fax: +39 079981044
info@hotelvillalastronas.it
www.hotelvillalastronas.it

Villa Luppis
Via San Martino, 34
33080 Rivarotta di Pasiano (Pordenone)
Tel. +39 0434626969
Fax: +39 0434626228
hotel@villaluppis.it
www.villaluppis.it

Villa Marsili
Viale C. Battisti
13 - 52044 Cortona (AR)
Tel. +39 0575605252
Fax: +39 0575605618
info@villamarsili.net
www.villamarsili.net

Villa Milani
Loc. Colle Attivoli, 4
06049 Spoleto
Tel. +39 0743225056
Fax: + 39 074349824
info@villamilani.com
www.villamilani.com

Villa Olmi Resort
Via degli Olmi 4/8
50012 Bagno a Ripoli
Florence
Tel. +39 055637710
Fax: +39 05563771600
info@villaolmiresort.com
www.villaolmiresort.com

RESTAURANTS

Antica Locanda del Falco
Castello Di Rivalta
Rivalta di Gazzola (Piacenza)
Tel. +39 0523978101
Fax: +39 0523978331
ilfalcodirivalta@libero.it
www.locandadelfalco.com

Ristorante IL Molino
Piazza Matteotti, 6/7
06038 - Spello (PG)
Tel. +39 0742651305
Fax: +39 0742302235
ristoranteilmolino@libero.it
www.palazzobocci.com/en/dining.html

La Bucaccia Ristorante
Via Ghibellina, 17 Cortona (AR)
Tel. / Fax: +39 0575606039
tipici@labucaccia.it
www.labucaccia.it

Ristorante Baita Ermitage
Localita Ermitage
Courmayeur (AO) - 11013
Tel. +39 016584435 1

Trattoria La Palomba
Via Cipriano Manente 16
05018 Orvieto
Tel. +39 0763343395
Fax: +39 0763343395

PARTNERS

Abitare La Storia
Sede di Presidenza e Segreteria
c/o Villa Dal Pozzo D'Annone
S.S. del Sempione, 5
28832 Belgirate (Verbania) Italia
Tel.+39 0322772156
Fax: +39 0322292678
Cell: +39 3463055743
mailbox@abitarelastoria.it
www.abitarelastoria.it

Gruppo Guide Alpine
Scuola di Alpinismo
Corso Italia 69/a "Ciasa de ra Regoles"
I-32043 Cortina d'Ampezzo (BL) Italy
Tel. / Fax: +39 0436868505
info@guidecortina.com
www.guidecortina.com

Italy Segway Tours
Segway Florence Srl
Address: Via de Servi 13, Florence, Italy
Tel. / Fax: +39 0552398855
info@italysegwaytours.com
www.italysegwaytours.co

PHOTO CREDITS

Front Cover: Top Left: The Cinque Terre's Vernazza is one of five villages nestled along Liguria's exquisite coastline and is perhaps the region's most enchanting. Top Right: Hotel Cenobio dei Dogi is located on the eastern Ligurian Riviera and is a short stroll from the charming fishing village of Camogli. Bottom Left: Venice's Palazzo Barbarigo Sul Canal Grande thrills visitors from the very first moments of approach. Bottom Right: Tombolo Talasso Resort is located within a small Mediterranean town on the Tuscan coast, where families can enjoy the beautiful beach.

Back Cover: Top Left & Right: Grand Hotel Excelsior Vittoria occupies a breathtaking location just off Sorrento's main square on a seaside cliff overlooking the Bay of Naples and Mount Vesuvius. Bottom Left: Hotel Ancora is located on the pedestrian mall that encircles the center of Cortina d'Ampezzo, one of the world's most famous resort towns. Bottom Center: Relais La Corte dei Papi's chefs will dazzle you as they prepare local Tuscan cuisine with a contemporary touch. Bottom right: Hotel Castello is one of seven hotels that compose the award-winning fifty-five-acre Forte Village Resort on the island of Sardinia.

Page 2: Val d'Aosta's Hotel Bellevue sits amid exquisite countryside bordering both Switzerland and France.

Page 4: The Mediterranean sea surrounding Sardinia is among the most beautiful and transparent in the entire world; the beach at Forte Village Resort.

Pages 6–7: At Castello di Vicarello, the body, mind, and soul instantly sense the extraordinary harmony of this magical place, making it an ideal vacation locale.

Pages 206–207: Relais & Chateaux Villa La Vedetta offers breathtaking views of Florence from its regal hilltop position high above the Arno on Piazzale Michelangelo and just a few steps from Ponte Vecchio.

Below: Publishers Debra and David Levinson at Hotel Pellicano d'oro in Sardinia.

To Our Readers: We at *Luxury Family Hotels & Resorts* extend a hearty thank-you to our readers for purchasing this guide. For those of you planning a visit to Italy, we hope it will help you journey more confidently with family members of all ages. If you are doing some armchair traveling, we hope these pages inspire you to one day soon join us in experiencing firsthand the magnificence that is Italy.

INDEX

Numbers in *italics* indicate photographs, maps, and charts.

Abano, 37
Abitare la Storia, 208–9
Abruzzo, 77, 87–89
Abruzzo National Park, 89
Acquaviva restaurant, 125
Aeolian archipelago, 13, 193
Agata e Romeo, 91
Agrigento, 172, 177
Alagna, 27
Alba, 30, 31
Albergo Pietrasanta, 92–93, 133
Alberobella, 165
Alberti, Davide, 47
Alghero, 174, 175, 204, 205
Alicudi, 172
Alighieri, Dante, 97, 135
Alpine Guide, 46, 47, 49
Altdeutsche Stube, 55
"al V piano" restaurant, 43
Amalfi, 164
Amalfi Coast, 168, 185
Am Hohen Feld Inn, 55
Amiata Mountains, 151
Ancient History Museum, 41
Ancona, 83
Anghelu Ruju Necropolis, 205
Antica Locanda del Falco, 77, 79, 137, 138–39
Antichita Miccio, 159
Antico Refettorio, 197
antipasti, 21
Aoelian Islands (Isole Eolie), 172, 192
Aosta, 27
Apeninne Mountains, 79, 87, 143
Apostelstube, 55
Apuglia. *See* Puglia
Arch of Augustus, 27
Archipelago Islands, 13
arch of Riccardo, 38
Arezzo, 81, 84, 97, 119, 127, 130, 153
Armani, Giorgio, 139
Arno River, 149
Artist's Tavern, 45
Ascoli Piceno, 83
Asparagus Festival, 61
Aspromonte National Park, 169
Assisi, 84, 105
Associazione Locali Storici d'Italia, 41
Attems Petzenstein Palace, 38
Auditorium Parco della Musica, 111

Automotive Museum, 29
Azzate, 66, 67

Baglioni Chapel, 113
Bagno a Ripoli, 159
Banini, Lucignanello, 89
Baptistery, 133
Bar à Fromage, 49
Barbaresco, 19, 21
Barbera, 21
Barchessa, 63
Bar delle Rose, 71
Bargello, 135
Bari, 165, 195
Barolo, 19, 21
Basilica di San Saturnino, 174
Basilica of St. Peter, 86
Basilicata, 167–69
Bassano del Grappa, 37, 60, 61
Battistero, 135
Baveno, 59
Bay of Naples, *162*, 163, 185, 212
Bay of Timi Ami, 201
Beauty Stop wellness center, 197
Beauvoir, Simone de, 91
Bellagio, 34
Bellini, 38
Belvedere Restaurant, 180, 182, 183
Bergamo, 34
Berti, Aurora, 101
Berti, Carlo Baccheschi, 101
Biferno, 89
Bioparco di Roma, 111
Bolgheri, 99
Bologna, 77–78, 79
Bolzano, 35, 55
Borghese Gardens, 109, 111
Borgo Antico, 123
Borgo Novo Suites, 123
Borgo Tre Rose, 82, *88*, 89, 94, 95
Borromeo Gulf, 59
Botanical Gardens, 41
Boutique, the, 197
Breakfast on the Beach, 93
Breganze, 35
Brenta River, 63, 65
Bressanone/Brixen, 35, 54, 55
Brixner Becken basin, 55
Brunelleschi, Filippo, 79
Brunello, 21
Buca Lapi, 133
Buonarroti House, 81

Ca' dei Frati, *37*, 73
Cagliari, 174, 178, 179, 180, 181, 182, 183, 201
Calabria, 168, 169–71, 172
Cala Gonone, 191
Cala Luna, 191
calazione (Italian breakfast), 24
Caltagirone, 177
Camogli, *30*, 31, *32*, 33, 52, 53, 56, 57, 212
Campania, 163–65, 168, 185
Campo di' Fiori, 86
Campobasso, 161
Cannes, 71
Canneto, 193
Capobianchi, Luigi, 155
Capri, 164, 185
Capulet house, 37
Carignano restaurant, 41
Carrara, 81, 93
Casa del Pittore, 123
Casino de la Vallée, 27
Castel Gandolfo Golf Club, 125
Castelli Romani hills, 86
Castello, 174
Castello del Buonconsiglo, 36
Castello di Gargonza, 96–97
Castello di Magona, 98–99
Castello di Montegridolfo, 123
Castello di Vicarello, *6–7*, *80*, 81, 100–101, 212
Castello Orsini Hotel, 102–3
Castelsardo, 174
Castle of Miramare, 38
Castle of Rivalta, 137
Catania, 172
Cathedral of San Giovanni, 29
Cathedral of San Giusto, 38
Cavalieri restaurant, 181
Cavalli, Elisabetta, 203
Caves of Matera, 168
Cavoli, 187
cena (dinner), 24
Central Italy, 77
  Abruzzo, 87–89
  Emilia-Romagna, 77–79
  Lazio, 86–87
  Marche, 82–84
  Tuscany, 79–82
  Umbria, 84–86
Cerveteri, 86
Cervinia, 27
Cetona Mountains, 151
Champoluc, 27
charts, 13
  driving distances, *17*

Chianti, 19, 82, 159
Chioggia, 37
Chiozza/Luppis family, 75
Church of San Clemente, 73
Church of Santa Maria Novella, 133
Cinque Terre, 33, 53, 57, 93
Cipriani Hotel, 38
Città di Castello, 84
Civitavecchia, 86
Cogne, 29, 48, 49
Colli Bolognesi, 79
Colli di Parma, 79
Colli Piacentini, 79
Colosseum, 86
Coluccia Peninsula, 189
Company Villa Grazioli, 125
Congregation of Hermit Fathers of Montelucco, 105
Corallina, 71
Corpus Domini feast, 113
Corsica, 189
Cortina, 45
Cortina d'Ampezzo, 37, 44, 45, 46, 212
Cortona, *23*, 81, 95, 130, 131, 144, 145, 150, 151, 152, 153
Costa Rei, 198, 199
Costa Smerelda, 174, 191
Costa Verde, 203
Courmayeur, 27, 50, 51
Cremona, 34
Crete Senesi, 121

Dal Corso, Alessandro, 63, 65
Dal Corso, Dario, 63, 65
Dal Corso family, 65
d'Ambra, Manuela Tiraboschi, 193
da Vinci, Leonardo, 79, 116
De Ferrari family, 53
Dei Dogi Restaurant, 53
di Massa, Ginesio del Barba, 105
DOC (*Denominazione di Origine Controllata*) certification, 20, 24
DOCG (*Denominazione di Origine Controllata e Garantia*) certification, 20
Doges (Genoese), 53
Dolcetto, 21
Dolomite Alps, *27*, 45, 47
DOP certification, 24
Dora Baltea River, 27
Doria Castle, 174
Ducal Palace, 34
Duomo, 133, 135
Duomo di Milano, 34

Egadi, 172
Egyptian Museum, 29
Elba, 81, 99
Emilia, 78
Emilia-Romagna, 20, 23, 77–79, 123, 137, 139
Enoteca Marcucci, 93
Eremo delle Grazie, 23, 104–5
Etruscan Arch, 84
Etruscan Museum of Villa Giulia, 111
Etruscan Well, 84

Falconara Charming House & Resort, *168, 170, 171, 176–77*
Fano, 83
Ferdinand (emperor of Austria), 55
Ferragamo family, 119
Ferrara, 77
Festival dei Due Mondi (Festival of Two Worlds), 84, 155
Festival della Canzone, 31
Filicudi, 172
Fiorentino family, 185
Fiori di Murano, 71
Florence/Firenze, 11, 24, 77, 79, 81, 92, 93, 99, 116, 117, 119, 121, 122, 127, 128, 129, 133, 134, 135, 141, 142, 143, 146, 147, 148, 149, 158, 159, 212
Flowers (Italian Riviera), 71
Forte dei Marmi, 81
Forte Village Resort, *10, 165,* 178–83, 212
Francesca, Piero della, 91
Frascati, 86, 87, 125
Fraterna Fountain, 163
French Riviera, 71
Friuli Venezia Giulia, 20, 38–39

Gabicce Mare, 83
Gaggini, Sebastiano, 57
Gaja, Angelo, 19
Galano, Vincenzo, 185
Galleria dell'Accademia, 81
Galleria Palatina, 81
Gargano Peninsula, 165
Garibaldi, 174
Genoa, 31, 55, 57
Giannutri, 99
Gibson, Mel, 195
Giglio, 99
Giotto, 37
Giotto's Campanile, 133
Giuseppe Verdi theatre, 38
Gli Arazzi, 73
Gli Specchi, 73
Golfo Aranci, 190, 191
Golfo dei Poeti (Poets Gulf), 33
Gorizia, 38
Gourmet del-l'Hotel Bellevue, 49
Grado, 39
Grand Hotel Excelsior Vittoria, *162, 163,* 184–85, 212
Grand Hotel Sitea, 40–41

Grand Visconti Palace, *33,* 42–43
Gran Paradiso, 27
Gran Paradiso national park, 29, 49
Grappa, 21, 24, 37
Grasparossa di Castelvetro, 79
Gressonney, 27
Grosseto, 81, 100, 101
Grotta dei Gridolfi, 123
Grotta della Foca, 165
Grottaferrata, 86, 124, 125
Grotta Palazzese, 165
Grotta Stalattitica, 165
Grunser, Viktor, 55
Gruppo Guide Alpine Cortina, 46–47
Gubbio, 84
Guerra, Camillo, 195
Gulf of Alghero, 205
Gulf of Baratti, 141
Gulf of Cagliari, 174
Gulf of Catania, 172
Guspini, 202, 203

Harry's Bar, 38
Heiss family, 55
Henderson, John, 157
Holistic Center La Serra, 185
Hotel Albergo del Sole al Pantheon, 90–91
Hotel Ancora, 44–45, 212
Hotel Bellevue, *2, 20, 34, 35,* 48–49, 212
Hotel Cala Caterina, *164,* 186–87
Hotel Castello at Forte Village Resort, 180–81
Hotel Cenobio Dei Dogi, *9, 30, 31, 32, 33,* 52–53, 57, 212
Hotel Dei Mellini, 106–7
Hotel Eden, *86, 87,* 108–9
Hotel Elephant, 34, 54–55
Hotel La Coluccia, *163, 175,* 188–89
Hotel Lord Byron, *81,* 110–11
Hotel Palazzo Bocci, *25,* 112–13, 115
Hotel Pellicano D'Oro, 190–91
Hotel Portofino Kulm, 56–57
Hotel Regency, 24, 78, 79, *87,* 116–17
Hotel Villa Aminta, *29,* 58–59
Hotel Villa Ca' Sette, 60–61
Hotel Villa Franceschi, *38,* 62–63, 65
Hotel Villa Margherita, *38,* 63, 64–65
Hotel Villa Meligunis, 192–93

I Ginepri, 201
IGT (*Indicazione Geografica Tipica*) certification, 20
Il Belvedere Restaurant, 199
Il Borro, 118–19
Il Caildario, 99
Il Cavaliere, 159
Il Cobezzolo, 199
Il Duomo, 34
Il Giardano dei Limoni, 197
Il Giardino, 71
Il Latini, 133
Il Mediterraneo, 201

Il Melograno Cooking School and Restaurant, 195
Il Melograno Relais & Chateaux, *11,* 167, 194–95
Il Pelagone golf club, 99
Il Ristoro, 123
Il Salotto Lounge & Wine Bar, 111
Il Verrocchio restaurant, 149
Infiorata, 113
International Operetta Festival, 38
Ischia, 164
Isernia, 161–63
Isola Bella, 34, 59
Isola dei Pescatori, 34, 59
Isola Madre, 59, 34
Italy
 categorizing wines' origin, 20
 culinary journey through, 23–24
 dining out in, 25
 diversity of, 9
 regional cuisines of, 23. *See also* regional cuisine
 wines of, 19–21. *See also* regional wines
 worldwide rankings in wine production, vineyards, and consumption, 19
Italy Segway Tours, 134–35
itinerary, designing, 13

Jewish Ghetto, 86
John (king of Portugal), 55

La Boutique, 73
La Bucaccia Ristorante, 19 , 20, *21,* 84, *85,* 151, 152, 153
La Grotta, 121
Lake Bracciano, 86
Lake Como, 34, 67
Lake Garda, 37
Lake Maggiore, 29, 30, 34, 59, 67
Lake Orta, 29
Lake Trasimeno, 84
Lake Varese, 67
La Laguna, 73
La Maddalena Archipelago, 174
Landi family, 137
La Perla della Laguna, 73
La Petite Restaurant, 49
La Playa restaurant, 53
La Rocchetta restaurant, 137
La Rosetta, 91
La Rotonda, 199
La Scala, 34
La Sila Grande, 169
Last Supper, The (Leonardo), 34
La Terrazza dell' Eden, *86,* 109
La Torre di Gargonza Restaurant, 91
La Valheureusa Wellness Oasis, 49
La Veranda (Hotel Villa Franceschi), 63
La Veranda (Sofitel Thalassa Timi Ama), 201
Lazio, 77, 86–87, 125, 163
le Brasserie du Bon Bec, 49

Lecce, 167
Le Conchiglie, 73
Le Isole, 59
Le Maschere, 73
Leopold II (grand duke of Tuscany), 99
Lerici, 33
Les Bougainvillees, 197
Le Tamerici Beach Club, 195
le Vallée Blanche ski school, 49
Levinson, Ari, 27
Levinson, David, *9, 13, 27, 212*
Levinson, Debra, *9, 13, 212*
Levinson, Isaac, *27,* 47
Levinson, Jacob, 27
Liguria, 31–33, 70
Ligurian, 33, 53, 57
Ligurian coast, 23, 27, 33, 53
Lipari, 172, 192, 193
Livenza River, 75
Livorno, 82, 98, 140
Locandi Dei Mai Intees, 66–67
L'Olivaia restaurant, 143
Lombardy, 33, 34–35, 43
Lombardy Alps, 67
L'Osteria del Borro, 119
Lucca, 79, 81, 93, 121, 127
Lucignanello Bandini, *89,* 120–21
Lucignano d'Asso, 121
Lucretili Mountains, 103
Lugana, 35
Luppis, Giorgio Ricci, 75
Luppis, Stefania, 75
Luppis family, 75
luxury, standards for, 9–10
Luxury Family team, 11
Luxury Family Travelers, perks for, 11

Macerata, 83
Maddalena Archipelago, 191
Madonna di Campiglio, 35
Magi, Agostina, 153
Magi, Franceschina, 153
Magi, Romano, 153
Maiella National Park, 89
Mancini, 91
Mantarro, Massimo, 172, 197
Mantova, 34
maps, 13
 Central Italy, *76*
 estimated driving times, *15*
 major airport locations, *16*
 major cities, provinces, roads, and water features, *14*
 Northern Italy, *26*
 Southern Italy, *161*
Marano Lagoon, 38–39
Maratea, 168
Marche, 77, 82–84, 123
Marchetto, Joel, 201
Maremma, 101
Margherita (queen mother), 57

Marina Corta, 193
Marostica, 37
Marquis de Sade, 125
Martini, Simone, 127
Mascagni, 91
Matterhorn, 27
Mayes, Frances, 151
Meacci, Stefano, 151
Medicean Bar & Pool Bar, 149
Medici Chapel, 81
Meduna River, 75
Meran/Merano, 35
Merano, 35
Mercial, Cesare, 99
Metaponto, 168
Michelangelo (Buonarroti), 9, 79, 81, 105, 206, 212
Michelozzi family, 143
Michelstaedter, Carlo, 38
Milan, 27, 31, 33, 34, 42, 43, 67
Milani, Giovanna, 155
Milani, Giovanni Battista, 155
Milani, Milena, 45
Mira Porte, 62, 63, 64, 65
Misano Adriatico, 77
Modena, 78
Modica, 177
Molas Golf Club, 179
Molise, 87, 161–63
Monopoli, 194
Montalcino, 81, 101, 121
Monte Blanc, 27
Monte-Carlo, 71
Monte Conero, 83
Montefalco, 86
Montefiascone, 87
Montepulciano, 20, 81, 82, 83, 84, 94, 95, 121
Monte Rosa, 27
Monte Rosa Massif, 67
Monte San Savino, 96, 97
Monticchio, 168
Mosaic School of Spilimbergo, 75
Mount Etna, 172
Mount Falterona, 143
Mount Grappa, 61
Mount Portofino, 53, 57
Mount Vesuvius, 162, 163, 164, 185
Mugello valley, 143
Museo degli Argenti (Silver Museum), 81
Museu Civico, 127
Museum of Capodimonte, 163
Museum of the Holy Shroud, 41
Museum of Santa Maria delle Monache, 163
Museum of the Synagogue, 38
Mysteries, the, 161

Naples, 163–64, 184, 185, 212
National Archaeological Museum, 163–64
National Gallery, 84
National Gallery of Modern Art, 111
National History Museum of Artillery, 41

National Museum of Cinema, 41
Navigli, 34
Navona Square, 91
Nebbiolo, 19, 21
Nice, 71
Nietzsche, Friedrich, 91
Northern Italy, 27
    Friuli Venezia Giulia, 38–39
    Liguria, 31–33
    Lombardy, 34–35
    Piedmonte, 29–31
    Trentino–Alto Adige, 35–36
    Valle d'Aosta, 27–29
    Veneto, 36–38
Not Just Jazz, 43

Olbia, 190, 191
Oleoteca (olive oil center), 143
Onice, 129
Oratoria dei Frati, 197
Orcia Valley, 121
Ormea, 33
Ornellaia, 19
Orsini Odescalchi castle, 86
Orvieto, 84, 105, 157
Osteria dell'Accademia, 123
osteria, 24
Ostia Antica, 86

Padova, 24
Padua, 37
Paestum, 164
Palazzo Aminto Beauty & Spa, 59
Palazzo Barbarigo Sul Canal Grande, 36, 68–69, 212
Palazzo Barberini, 111
Palazzo Barsanti Bonetti, 93
Palazzo Comunale, 157
Palazzo Niccolini-Bourbon, 133
Palazzo Pitti, 81
Palazzo Viviani, 122–23
Palermo, 172
Palio horse race, 81, 127
Palladio, Andrea, 37, 61
Panarea, 172
panineria, 24
Pannini, Giovanni Paolo, 125
Pantelleria, 172
Pantheon, 86, 91, 107
Papi, David, 131
Papi family, 131
Parco dell' Uccellina, 99
Pardini, Barbara, 93, 133
Parioli Quarter, 111
Park Hotel Villa Grazioli, 124–25
Parma, 78
Parsifal (Wagner), 164
Pascara, 167
Pasquali, Paolo, 143
Passerini, Silvio, 145
pasta, types of, unique to Italy's regions, 23

Pelagie Islands, 172
Pennucci, Rino, 117
Perugia, 84, 105
Pesaro, 83
Pevero Club, 191
Piacenza, 77, 136, 137, 138, 139
Piacenza hills, 79
Piazza, Marco, 139
Piazza, Sabrina, 139
Piazza Armerina, 177
Piazza Cavour, 34
Piazza degli Strozzi, 135
Piazza del Campo, 81, 127
Piazza della Republica, 135
Piazza della Rotonda, 91
Piazza della Signoria, 135
Piazza del Popolo (Square of the People), 83, 111
Piazza family, 139
Piazza Farnese, 86
Piazza Navona, 86, 107
Piazza San Marco, 69
Piazza Vecchia, 34
Piazzale Roma, 69
Piazzetta, 123
Piccolomini family, 121
Piedmonte, 19, 20, 24, 29–31, 33, 40
Pietrasanta, 81, 92, 93, 132, 133
Pila, 27
Pinacoteca Nazionale, 127
Pinturicchio, frescoes of, 113
Pisa, 77, 79, 81, 93, 99, 119, 121, 127, 141
Pitigliano, 81
pizzeria, 24
Plose Mountain, 35
Policoro, 168
Polignano a Mare, 165
Pollino National Park, 169–71
pomace, 21
Pomati, Carlotta, 67
Pomati, Paolo, 67
Pomati family, 67
Pompeii, 164
Pondel Roman bridge, 49
Ponte Vecchio, 129, 135, 149
Porcellino, 135
porcini mushroom, 21, 30
Pordenone, 74
Po River Valley, 34, 78
Porta Romana, 43
Porto Cervo, 174
Portofino, 33, 53, 57, 71, 93
Porto Guinco, 187
Porto Rotondo, 174, 191
Portovenere, 33
Positano, 164
Praiano, 164
pranzo (lunch), 24
Prateria dell'Orso, 49
Principe Cerami Restaurant, 172, 197
Procida, 164

Puccini Opera Festival, 93
Puglia, 11, 24, 163, 165–67, 171, 195

Quagliarella, Andrea, 149

Ragusa, 172
Ragusa Ibla, 177
Rapallo, 33, 57
Ravello, 164
Ravenna, 77
Recasens, Patrick, 201
Reggiano, 79
Reggio, 78
Reggio dell'Emilia, 78
regional cuisine
    Abruzzo, 89
    Basilicata, 168
    Calabria, 171
    Campania, 164
    Emilia-Romagna, 78
    Friuli Venezia Giulia, 39
    Lazio, 86–87
    Liguria, 33
    Lombardy, 34–35
    Marche, 83
    Molise, 163
    Piedmonte, 30
    Puglia, 167
    Sardinia, 175
    Sicily, 172–73
    Trentino–Alto Adige, 36
    Tuscany, 81–82
    Umbria, 84
    Valle d'Aosta, 29
    Veneto, 37–38
regional wines
    Abruzzo, 89
    Basilicata, 169
    Calabria, 171
    Campania, 165
    Emilia-Romagna, 78–79
    Friuli Venezia Giulia, 39
    Lazio, 87
    Liguria, 33
    Lombardy, 35
    Marche, 83–84
    Molise, 163
    Piedmonte, 30–31
    Puglia, 167
    Sardinia, 175
    Sicily, 173–74
    Trentino–Alto Adige, 36
    Tuscany, 82
    Umbria, 86
    Valle d'Aosta, 29
    Veneto, 38
Relais Campo Regio, 126–27
Relais & Châteaux Villa la Vedetta, 128–29, 206–7, 212
Relais la Corte dei Papi, 82, 130–31, 212
Relais Le Jardin, 24, 78, 79, 87, 117

Residenza Del Moro, 92, 132–33
Residenza Torre di San Martino, 136–37
Restaurant I Mori, 59
Restaurant La Corte dei Papi, 82, 131, 212
Rialto Bridge, 69
Rimini, 77
Ristorante Baita Ermitage, 50–51
Ristorante Ca' 7, 61
Ristorante Il Molino, 25, 113, 114–15
Ristorante La Bucaccia, *19*, 20, *21*, 84, *85*, 151, 152–53
Ristorante Margherita, *38*, 63, 65
ristoranti (restaurant), 24
Ritrovo del Vecchio Forno, 123
Riva del Garda, 35
Rivalta, 137
Riviera di Levante, 31, 33
Riviera di Ponente, 31
Rivoli Castle, 41
Romagna, 78
Romagnan hills, 79
Roman Arena, 37
Roman Forum, 86
Roman Theatre (Valle d'Aosta), 27
Roman theatre (Friuli Venezia Giulia), 38
Rome, 11, 77, 81, 86–87, 90, 91, 102, 103, 106, 107, 108, 109, 110, 111, 124, 125, 145, 157
Rooms of the Planets, 81
Rossi, Paolo Alberto, 121
Roullet, Jeantet, 49
Rovereto, 35
Royal Armory, 29
Royal Hotel Sanremo, *31*, 70–71
Royal Palace, 29–30
Royal Wellness, 71
Russo, Andrea, 91

Sabauda Gallery, 29
Saint Isac, 105
Saint-Vincent, 27
Sala Corallo restaurant, 141
Salamino di Santa Croce, 79
Salina, 172
Salone Visconti, 43
Salviati, Roberto Guicciardini Corsi, 91
San Benedetto del Tranto, 83
San Clemente Island, 73
San Clemente Palace Hotel & Resort, 36, 37, 72–73
San Domenico Palace Hotel, *161*, *171*, *172*, 196–97
San Gimignano, 81, 121
San Marino, 77
San Martino Ripea Ruptae, 75
Sanctuary of St. Cosma and St. Damian, 163
Sangiovese, 19
Sanna Museum, 205
Sanremo, 31, 70, 71
Sanremo Casino, 71
Sant'Elmo Beach Hotel, 198–99
Sant'Elmo Grill Terrace, 199

Santa Crocie, 135
Santa Margherita di Pula, 178, 180, 182,
Santa Margherita Ligure, 53, 57
Santa Maria del Fiore, 133
Santa Maria di Tergu, 174
Santa Maria Maggiore, 113
Santa Teresa di Gallura, 174, 188, 189
Sapori del Lord Byron, 81, 111
Sardinia, 9, 11, 161, 163, 172, 174–75, 178, 179, 180, 181, 182, 183, 186, 187, 188, 189, 190, 191, 198, 199, 200, 201, 202, 203, 205, 212
Sardinian Archaeological Museum, 174
Sartor, Flavia, 45
Sartor, Renato, 45
Sartre, Jean-Paul, 91
Sassicaia, 19
Saturnia, 81
Scicli, 177
Senigallia, 83
Serpentara, 187
Sesone, Sergio, 34, 49
Sestri, 33
Settignano, 147
Sicily, 13, 23, 161, *170*, 171–74, 176, 177, 196, 197
Siena, 77, 79, 81, 99, 101, 119, 121, 126, 127
Sistine Chapel, 86, 109
Sofitel Thalassa Timi Ama, *172*, *173*, *174*, 175, 200–201
Sorbara, 79
Sorrentino, Nicola, 59
Sorrento, *162*, 163, 164, 184, 185, 212
South Tyrol, 35, 54
South Tyrol Museum of Archaeology, 35
Southern Italy, 161
  Basilicata, 167–69
  Calabria, 169–71
  Campania, 163–65
  Molise, 161–63
  Puglia, 165–67
  Sardinia, 174–75
  Sicily, 171–74
Spanish Steps, 86, 91, 107, 109, 111
Spello, 84, 112, 113, 114
Spoleto, *22*, 23, 25, 84, 104, 105, 154, 155
St. Mark's Square, 73
St. Peter's Cathedral (Isernia), 163
St. Peter's Cathedral (Rome), 107
St. Peter's Square, 86
Stibbert's museum, 81
Stresa, 30, 58, 59
Stromboli, 172
Südtirol, 35
Sulmona, 89
Syracuse, 172

Taormina, 13, 161, 172, 196, 197
Tarquinia, 86
Tarthesh Hotel, *8*, *9*, *166*, 167, 202–3
Tavolara Island, 191
Tenuta Tre Rose, *88*, *89*, 95

Termoli, 167
Thaermae del Forte spa, 181, 183
Thaermae del Forte Village, 179
Tignanello, 19
Tigullio Gulf, 33
Tivoli, 86
Todi, 84
Tombolo Talasso Resort, 140–41, 212
Tombolo Thalassotherapy Center and Spa, 141
Tornabuoni, 135
Trasimeno Lake, 151
Trastevere, 86
trattoria, 24
Trattoria Garga, 133
Trattoria La Palomba, 156–57
Trattoria Sciame, 121
Trebbiano, 21
Trebbia Valley, 137
Tremezzo, 34
Tremiti Islands, 167
Trentino–Alto Adige, *34*, 35–36
Trento, 24, 35, 36
Trento/Trentino, 35–36
Trevi Fountain, 86, 91, 107, 111
Trevignano, 86
Treviso, 24, 37
Trieste, 38
truffles, 30
trullis, 165
Turin, 29, 31, 40, 41
Tuscany (*Toscana*), 13, 19, 24, 77, 79–82, 93, 95, 97, 99, 101, 118, 119, 123, 131, 141, 143, 145, 147
Tusculum Hill, 125
Tyrrhenian Sea, 86, 125, 187

Uffizi, 79,
Uffizi Gallery, 133
Uffizi-Ponte Vecchio, 135
Umbria, 12, 13, 23, 77, 84–86, 105, 113, 115, 131, 145, 155, 157
Under the Tuscan Sun (Mayes), 151
Urbino, 83
Ustica, 172

Val d'Aosta, 20, 49, 51, 212
Valdichiana, 151, 153
Valle d'Aosta, 27–29
Valle dei Templi, 177
Valnerina, 105
Valpolicella, 37
Valtournenche, 27
Varenna, 34
Vatican City, 86, 107
VdT (*Vino da Tavola*) certification, 20–21
Venafro amphitheatre, 163
Veneto, 20, 24, 36–38, 45,
Venice, 11, 27, 36, 37, 38, 39, 60, 61, 62, 63, 64, 65, 68, 69, 72, 73, 75
Vermentino, 21

Versilia, 93
Via Condotti, 109
Via della Sapienza, 127
Viareggio, 81
Via Salaria, 103
Via Veneto, 86, 109, 111
Vicento, 24
Vicenza, 37
Viennese Terrace café, 45
Villa Aminta, *29*, 58–59
Villa Borghese, 86
Villa Campestri, 142–43
Villa Cimbrone, 164
Villa d'Este, 86
Villa del Casale, 177
Villa Del Parco & Spa at Forte Village Resort, 179, 182–83
Villa di Piazzano, *12*, 13, *18*, 19, *25*, 144–45
Villa Franceschi, 38
Villa Gamberaia, 146–47
Villa La Massa, 148–49
Villa Las Tronas, *169*, 204–5
Villa Luppis, *39*, 74–75
Villa Margherita, 38
Villa Marsili, 21, 150–51
Villa Milani, 154–55
Villa Olmi Resort, 158–59
Villa Palladiana, 63
Villa Rufolo, 164
Villasimius, 186, 187, 199, 200, 201
vin de pays, 20
Vineria Cacioteca, 153
Vino Noble di Montipulciano, 19
Visavis bar, 43
Viterbo, 86
Vittoria bar and restaurant, 185
Vittoria Terrace, 185
Vulcano, 172

Wimpole family, 145
wine, Italian. *See also* regional wines
  classifications of, 20–21
  improving variety and quality of, 19
  lacking legal standing until mid-1990s, 19
  pairing with food, 21
  red grapes, 19
  white grapes, 19

Zanetta family, 59
Zanieri, Roberto, 143
Zeffirino family, 57
Zeffirino Kulm, 57
Zirbelstube, 55
Zonta family, 61